Standards, Assessment, & Accountability

Standards, Assessment, & Accountability

Real Questions *from* Educators

WITH REAL ANSWERS FROM
DOUGLAS B. REEVES, Ph.D.

LEAD+
LEARN
PRESS

The Leadership and Learning Center
317 Inverness Way South, Suite 150
Englewood, Colorado 80112
Phone 1.866.399.6019 | Fax 303.504.9417
www.LeadandLearn.com

Published by Lead + Learn Press, a division of Advanced Learning Centers, Inc.

All Web links in this book are correct as of the publication date below but may have become inactive or otherwise modified since that time. If you notice a deactivated or changed link, please notify the publisher and specify the Web link, the book title, and the page number on which the link appears so that corrections may be made in future editions.

Lead+Learn Press also publishes books in a variety of electronic formats. Some content that appears in print may not be available in electronic books.

Library of Congress Cataloging-in-Publication Data

Reeves, Douglas B., 1953–
    Standards, assessment & accountability : real questions from educators, with real answers from Douglas B. Reeves, Ph.D. / Douglas B. Reeves.
        p. cm.
    Rev. ed. of: 101 questions & answers about standards, assessment, and accountability, c2001.
    Includes bibliographical references and index.
    ISBN 978-1-933196-94-7
    1. Education--Standards--United States--Miscellanea. 2. Education--United States--Evaluation--Miscellanea. 3. Educational accountability--United States--Miscellanea. I. Reeves, Douglas B., 1953- 101 questions & answers about standards, assessment, and accountability. II. Title. III. Title: Standards, assessment, and accountability.
    LB3060.83.R44 2010
    379.1'580973--dc22
                                                                                    2010022955

ISBN 978-1-933196-94-7

Printed in the United States of America

14 13 12 11 10   01 02 03 04 05 06 07

About the Author

 **Douglas B. Reeves, Ph.D.**

Dr. Douglas Reeves is the founder of The Leadership and Learning Center. He has worked with education, business, nonprofit, and government organizations throughout the world. The author of more than twenty books and many articles on leadership and organizational effectiveness, he has twice been named to the Harvard University Distinguished Authors Series. Dr. Reeves was named the Brock International Laureate for his contributions to education. He also received the Distinguished Service Award from the National Association of Secondary School Principals and the Parents Choice Award for his writing for children and parents.

Other Lead + Learn Press
Publications by Dr. Douglas Reeves

Contents

Preface

How the Questions and Answers Were Created

The questions in this text are from real teachers, administrators, parents, and board members in schools around the world. They represent a fraction of the thousands of correspondents who have been kind enough to seek my advice in the past few years. While my responses may frequently fall short of the mark, my intent has been to offer candor and practicality. The questions have been edited for length and to protect the identity of the writer. The responses have been edited to provide necessary references and, I hope, the clarity which I failed to include in the first draft of my correspondence. Otherwise, the reader will see the dialog precisely as it was initially created.

Standards

When the first edition of *101 Questions & Answers about Standards, Assessment, and Accountability* was published, the United States was slowly moving toward a standards-based educational environment. After more than two centuries of idiosyncratic academic expectations, a growing number of states established clear and specific criteria for what students should know and be able to do. While other industrialized nations achieved a national consensus about academic expectations for students, the United States clung tenaciously to the notion of "local control," a doctrine that has deep roots in the Tenth Amendment to the United States Constitution. That amendment, which is part of the Bill of Rights, expresses, innocently enough, the doctrine that powers not enumerated in the Constitution are reserved to the states or the people. In other words, if the Constitution does not discuss public education, then it is a matter in which the federal government may not become involved.

While I have deep reverence for the original text of the Constitution, this document also disenfranchised women and counted a slave as 60 percent of a person. Over the course of time, revolution, war, and reconciliation, we have learned that education, along with other fundamental human rights, is not merely a matter of local interest, but one in which the entire society has an interest. For example, the Supreme Court eventually ruled that "local control" did not mean that individual school districts were empowered to provide "separate but equal" education to students based on their ethnicity. As this book goes to press, 48 of the 50 states have agreed to pursue "common core" standards. This does not mean that local jurisdictions have relinquished their unique perspectives on teaching and learning. It *does* mean that the alphabet has the same number of letters in Massachusetts and Missouri, and that the square of the hypotenuse is equal to the sum of the squares of the other sides of a right triangle in both Indiana and Iowa.

Assessment

The focus of assessment has shifted dramatically from summative to formative assessment. While year-end summative assessments remain of vital importance, a growing number of jurisdictions have embraced the need for formative assessments. Popham and Marzano remind us that an assessment is not "formative" because of the label, but rather because of the way in which it is used. If an assessment fails to inform instruction and learning, then it is not formative, but merely another test. Hattie (2009) reminds us that formative assessment is one of the most powerful techniques that educators can use to improve student achievement. In this volume, my correspondents express a significantly increased interest in formative assessment.

Accountability

While standards and assessment have progressed over the years, accountability has not. The United States and many other nations continue to equate accountability with student test scores. Policy makers appear to be eager to hold nine-year-old children accountable, but are inexplicably reluctant to apply the same criteria to adults. The persistent missing link in educational policy around the world is the fundamental moral principle that no child in any educational system will be more accountable than the adults who presume to govern it. Therefore, this book is inherently incomplete, as it responds to prevailing notions of accountability. The job is only half begun when we discuss accountability in terms of student test scores, and even, in a few more progressive places, the performance of teachers and principals. This book series will be retired when there are standards, assessment, and accountability systems in place for legislators, parliamentarians, members of Congress, and other officials around the world. Retirement for this series (and its writer) is, I suspect, elusive.

I am indebted to my colleagues Katie Schellhorn and Cathy Shulkin for their expert assistance in assembling and editing this manuscript. Most of all, I offer my appreciation to teachers, administrators, students, parents, and policy makers around the world who took the time to write to me. I hope that my responses constitute, not an answer, but at least the beginning of a dialog that will continue long into the future.

DOUGLAS B. REEVES
Nahant, Massachusetts
April 2010

The Leadership and Learning Center

Schools are busy places. Decisions we make on a daily basis are part of an integrated, holistic system centered on student learning. We must focus on what to teach, how to teach it, and how to meet individual student needs. We must also be confident these strategies work. The Leadership and Learning Center's clear and focused purpose is to improve student achievement by increasing the knowledge and skills of educators.

Founded by Dr. Douglas Reeves as the Center for Performance Assessment, The Leadership and Learning Center is a professional development organization that works with schools throughout the world, specifically on issues regarding standards, assessment, and accountability. Although The Center's primary work continues to be with public school systems, we regularly work with independent and charter schools, community colleges and universities, state departments of education, national ministries of education, and international educational associations.

The Center serves educators through professional development, publishing, and consulting. We provide professional-development seminars, trainings, and conferences for teachers, school leaders, and policy makers. We specialize in professional development focused on issues of accountability, standards-based assessment, effective teaching strategies, leadership, and data analysis. In addition, we provide seminars specifically adapted for the needs of English language learners and special education students.

To support capacity-building for our clients, The Center publishes and distributes resources, including books, videos, audiobooks, posters, and other tools for teachers, leaders, and parents. Some of The Center's best-known works include *Making Standards Work* and *Accountability in Action* by Dr. Douglas Reeves; *Power Standards* and *"Unwrapping" the Standards* by Larry Ainsworth; *Beyond the Numbers* and *Show Me the Proof!* by Dr. Stephen White; *Compelling Conversations* by Dr. Thomasina Piercy; and *Ready for Anything* by Lynn Howard (all published by Lead + Learn Press). The Center also provides personalized consulting services, including the development of accountability systems, creation of assessment systems, research, evaluation, coaching, and individualized services designed to meet the unique needs of each client.

CHAPTER 1

Standards

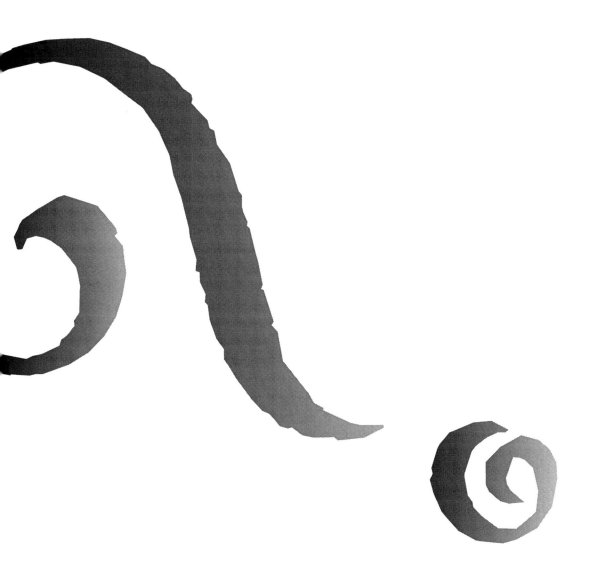

Standards

Can you suggest how to approach the establishment of standards for language arts in grades K–6 for an independent school?

The key to creating standards for any school, including independent schools, is to answer the question, "What do we want students to know and be able to do by the time that they leave our school?" For many independent schools, the answer is, "We want to give our students the choice to attend college, including the nation's most elite universities." That has some serious implications for the K–12 curriculum.

The typical initial result of the standards-setting process is academic gluttony—giving every suggestion from every source equal weight and declaring that they all look good. Indeed, they all *do* look good, provided that you have a 400-day school year. If you are at the beginning of this process, you can avoid the mistake so many other schools have made and focus on essentials, rather than accumulating a burdensome and unrealistic list of standards.

I would especially recommend Larry Ainsworth's books *Power Standards* and *"Unwrapping" the Standards*. My book *Making Standards Work* may also be helpful.

The other mistake that schools typically make is establishing standards without considering what the implications are for curriculum, assessment, and schedule. If you decide, as I hope that you will, that students need to do substantially more nonfiction writing, along with editing, rewriting, and collaborative scoring, it is insufficient to merely establish a declaration of this standard. You must also consider how to assess writing in a consistent manner in every class, how to create time for writing (doubling the time allocated to English language arts would be a good start), and how to give teachers time for collaborative scoring. Too many schools continue to operate on the false quality model of "It had better be right the first time." The real quality model is that work is submitted, then students receive feedback, then students respect and use that feedback to improve performance.

Q 2

In my school district, many of us are ready to implement the process you describe in *Making Standards Work*, but there are also many teachers in my high school and district who resist it. Some of the resistance is legitimate and some is not—we have to deal with both. I think you will agree that the teachers can make the process succeed or fail. We've come too far and achieved too many goals to have it fail now because we push too hard or too fast.

Common semester finals were introduced several years ago, with the agreement between the teachers association and the school administrators that the results would not be used for evaluation. Since then, we have used the results as a way to compare the teachers to the average in the school district for the subject and level they teach. The teachers resent this. They always have good excuses for their ranking, and someone has to be in the bottom fifty percent. Reports with item analysis that teachers could find useful were available, but were not emphasized. Not until last year, with the implementation of the Edusoft® Assessment Management System, did the teachers have accessible data that they could use to improve learning. At my school, some departments have created common quarterly assessments that allow them to discuss results, but they do not like to share the results with the administration unless it's done informally with someone they trust. WestEd is now creating common benchmark assessments that all schools in our district will have to use when they don't meet Adequate Yearly Progress (AYP). The bottom line is that teachers see the value of assessments that test common learning, and they even share common assessments that they design at the site level for their students each year, but they do not want more common assessments from the district.

Four years ago, our teachers were resisting the use of standards. Now they have committed to teaching the standards. There is a dialogue about what standards mean, Power Standards, and aligning test items to standards. We are seeing improved Academic Performance Index (API) results. There is buy-in for the standards among teachers. We don't want this progress to be undermined by forcing common benchmark assessments from the top down.

A presenter from The Leadership and Learning Center said that the goal would be to have monthly common assessments. Our teachers think that this is too many, and that they are *too* common. Good teachers need to be able to adjust their teaching to their students, who are different each year. If the teachers must teach for monthly, common, external, benchmark exams they will not adjust, review, and personalize their teaching. And worst of all, morale will be low, because teachers will not have input in the assessment process, so they won't buy in to it.

For now, should we be satisfied with getting teachers to consider common Power Standards and performance tasks? We can let them grade based on Power Standards, and provide them with time to discuss the results of their own assessments of these common standards. Some of these assessments may be common at the site level. We could facilitate this by training teachers to use Edusoft®, so they can create and store common assessment items that they can use to test the Power Standards. Teachers will be more likely to accept the common assessment concept if it grows from the bottom up.

 First, congratulations on your move to common semester finals. That's a terrific step in the right direction, and shows that the teacher's association and school administrators can work collaboratively toward the very important goal of equity and common expectations for all students. Special congratulations to the teachers who have created common quarterly assessments. Teacher-created assessments will be more strongly linked to the curriculum than those created by others. If those assessments are strongly linked to state standards, and are closely related to what is expected of students on the state tests, then we encourage you to use those assessments, not replace them. Whatever help you get from outside organizations on assessment development, I would hope that teacher participation and ownership would remain a strong part of assessment design.

I certainly do not follow the logic of using two different sets of common assessments, one for those who meet AYP and one for those who don't. If you do that, you no longer have "common" assessments. The entire premise of common assessments is that every student will have the same expectations.

If data analysis is done primarily for the purpose of negative evaluations and rankings, then I'm not surprised that teachers do not embrace it. I think it is a much better strategy to use data analysis as a "treasure hunt," identifying excellent teaching practices and relentlessly focusing on positive work and also praising gains, even when final results are not yet where you would like them to be.

That said, I am not sure I understand why any employee would not want to share assessments or assessment results. Collaboration is a necessity in any effective school, and transparency is a requirement for fairness. I endorse what you said about teacher involvement in the creation of Power Standards and common assessments. But it's not an either/or situation—both are needed. In fact, if teachers work together on Power Standards first, it makes the task of creating common assessments much easier.

Finally, I think you should give your district and your teachers an enormous amount of credit for what has already been accomplished and the progress that has been made. Celebrate that—but don't stop now. Standards without assessments mean nothing. Assessments that are inconsistent from one class to the next, one school to the next, and one neighborhood to the next, are unfair. Don't stop until you can look every student in the eye and say, "I have the same expectations for you as I do for the wealthiest kid in town."

 What advice regarding standards-based curriculum do you have for teachers working with students who have learning disabilities and behavior disorders, in co-teaching situations where students' achievement levels vary greatly?

 The key to success in *any* classroom, and particularly in those with the diverse learning needs that you have described, is effective differentiation of instruction. While we may want all students to write a paragraph, for example, some students can do that in a single session, while learning-disabled students may require multiple sessions that include using pictures and graphic organizers, creating main ideas and bullet points, writing a sentence or two, and, ultimately—perhaps after several days or weeks—writing a paragraph.

Standards do not mean standardization of the lesson. Standards simply provide a target for achievement that applies to every student.

One of the most common special education techniques is incremental instruction, and I would argue that it is not so much "special" education as it is "good" education—something that must be done for every student.

One more idea to consider is the multi-task assessment, which should be designed in such a way that foundational learning needs, including those below the present grade level, are taken into account, and, in later tasks, highly challenging problems beyond the present grade level are also available. All students can be working on the same set of standards, using the same scenario, but they can be working on different tasks at the same time. There are several examples of multi-task assessments in the appendices of my book *Making Standards Work.*

Our state is talking about requiring standards-based education for all students. In my district, where I am the program director for Literacy Education, we are at the ground level. We are asking "Why standards?" and "How do you teach to standards?" I have read your book *Making Standards Work.* Can you recommend articles about the reasoning behind standards-based education that will enable our educators to clearly understand it? I have been using the Final Word Protocol to deepen our discussions. Any advice addressing additional strategies to use during our investigation would be helpful.

I think you've nailed the essence of the issue—the *reason* that teachers will embrace standards has nothing to do with federal or state law, but rather is a reflection of the ethical, moral, and professional rationale for standards.

Some additional resources you might want to consider:

- *"Unwrapping" the Standards* and *Power Standards* by Larry Ainsworth. Both books are available through The Leadership and Learning Center. We also offer free book study guides for faculties that want to do book studies.

- My article in *Education Week*, "If You Hate Standards, Learn to Love the Bell Curve," also is related to this issue. It is available at www.edweek.org.
- Grant Wiggins wrote a wonderful article about this issue in *Educational Leadership* titled "Standards, Not Standardization."

I want to compare scores from a non-standards-based curriculum to scores on our new performance standards. What information can I expect to get from this comparison? How can I use this existing data to tell if the standards-based curriculum is working or increasing student achievement in reading? Can I use some kind of statistics to tell me more (by entering the data into a statistical analysis package such as SPSS)?

Whether you use SPSS or Microsoft Excel or just a hand-written data set, here are the key points to bear in mind:

First, be sure to make a "same-student-to-same-student" comparison. In other words, it is of some value to compare last year's third grade students to this year's third grade students. Perhaps the differences in scores will be due to the differences in curriculum. But perhaps the differences in scores will be due to the fact that they are different children. It is therefore far more persuasive to have pre- and post-test data for the same group of children that shows the gains that they made with treatment A (the previous curriculum) compared to the gains that they made with treatment B (the new curriculum). You would expect both data sets to show gains—after all, the kids were in school. But your hypothesis is that the gains would be of a different magnitude.

Second, if you are examining effects across many different classrooms, then it is imperative to acknowledge that there is more going on than the presence or absence of a new curriculum. In every curriculum or teaching reform, the fundamental issue is *degree of implementation*. I have seen new reading curricula implemented in a single school with some classrooms devoting 90 minutes each day, others devoting 120 minutes each day, and others devoting 180 minutes each day to the "same" curriculum. I have also seen many schools claiming to have the same new curriculum, but the actual use and implementation varied widely between schools. When researchers tracked the actual degree of use of the new curriculum, they found that low levels of implementation were worse than no change at all, and only the highest levels of implementation were effective. This will help you avoid the "brand name fallacy," in which vendors attempt to claim that the brand name of the curriculum is the salient variable in student achievement. You and I know that teaching, leadership, and daily implementation are far more important.

My district is moving towards a standards-based approach in mathematics. Has there been any definitive work regarding whether standards-based reform curricula are more effective than a traditional approach? I have read lots of research on both sides, but it is difficult to figure out which research is the most sound. I would like to find some unbiased work, not research supported by the more radical groups. I am looking for something that does not have an agenda. I was wondering if you might be able to guide me in the right direction.

You are quite right that some of the opinions (certainly more opinion than research) on both sides of the question are so strident and extreme that they strain credulity. But there are some reasoned middle-ground sources to consider.

I would start with the work of Robert J. Marzano and John S. Kendall (1996, 1998), The book *Standards for Our Schools: How to Set Them, Measure Them, and Reach Them*, by Marc S. Tucker and Judy B. Codding (1998), made a similar case. There is a series of pertinent articles in the periodical *K–16 Connection*, available at www.EdTrust.org (Haycock, 1998). I would also consider the work of Grant Wiggins; his book *Educative Assessment* (1998) comes to mind, as well as his more recent work with Jay McTighe in *Understanding by Design*, published in association with the ASCD. My own book *Making Standards Work* might also be helpful. You will find in these books citations of the work of other researchers, including Ruth Mitchell, who has studied standards both in the United States and abroad.

What I think is most important in your consideration of these arguments, however, is the alternative. Your question suggests that the alternative to standards is a traditional approach. More specifically, the alternative to standards is the bell curve—either we compare students to an objective standard or we compare them to each other (see my 2001 article in *Education Week*, "If You Hate Standards, Learn to Love the Bell Curve.") I think we can admit that standards suffer from many deficiencies—there are too many of them, they are insufficiently specific (or, in some states, *too* specific), they are poorly linked to assessment, and they are inadequately taught. Even as we concede all of those problems, at the end of the day I would conclude—in mathematics and every other discipline—that it is far more effective to compare a student's work to an objective standard than to say, "He doesn't know how to apply the Pythagorean Theorem, but he's not as bad as the other kids, so he passes." That's exaggerating the point, but only slightly. Bell-curve classes will always call some kids "above average" and "successful," even if they are not proficient. Bell-curve classes will always call some kids "below average" and "failures," even if they are proficient.

Finally, consider the use of standards elsewhere in society—driver's licenses, pilot's exams, brain surgery boards, hygiene inspections at fast food restaurants. All of them use standards, not bell-curve comparisons.

Q7

My district is working on identifying Power Indicators and using pacing guides and Short Cycle Assessments in all core subjects. The staff (in general) is very receptive and loves the work we are having them do. As a matter of fact, we have quickly seen great growth in student achievement and buy-in as we move through these processes. But one high school science teacher challenged the whole idea of Power Standards, saying that by doing this, we are not helping the highest level thinker get to the next level. This teacher suggested that we are, in fact, hindering advanced students from scoring at the highest possible levels in Advanced Placement classes, on AP tests, and even on ACT and SAT exams.

It's an interesting hypothesis—that having students gain deeper knowledge of a subject will hinder them on an AP test. The only way to deal with a hypothesis is to test it, using two different classes with two similar groups of students and either the same teacher or two teachers with roughly equal histories of students passing the AP tests.

Teacher A covers everything—which, if AP supplementary readings and content are taken seriously, should require a good two years. In fact, *every* AP teacher I know makes some choices about what is most important, and does not cover everything. Those choices may not be called "Power Standards," but they are still choosing what to teach, and what not to teach.

Teacher B analyzes the curriculum, identifies the subjects that are most important for students, and seeks to have all students gain proficiency.

In the first class, it's sink or swim. In the second class, if students fail a lab or a test, they do it again.

The first class may claim to be more rigorous, but the second class actually requires more work, and usually results in better learning. I think one of the big myths about Power Standards is that by addressing fewer elements of content, students are not working as hard and are not challenged as much. That is not true. Deep understanding of science or any other field requires much more work and higher-level thinking. I have never said that adopting Power Standards means that students do not have to learn facts. Chemistry, statistics, and history all require factual knowledge in addition to deep understanding. Students also need *very* heavy doses of writing—clear, college-level writing. It's not an either/or proposition.

But you don't have to take my word for it. Let the data speak for itself. Find two volunteers, perhaps even in two different subjects. Have one teacher continue teaching in the traditional manner, while the other tries using Power Standards. Give students a mock AP test at the beginning of the class and a comparable test at the end of the class, and see who gains the most. Test all of the students with the real AP test if you can. Draw your own conclusions.

If both classes do equally well, then you might want to the chose the curriculum that is more rational and has greater ownership by the teachers who created it. Curriculum based on Power Standards almost always fits those criteria as well.

How can we begin to make our schools more performance-based for students when our state really hasn't defined what the performance standards and the learning standards should be?

I'm aware that some states have resisted establishing performance standards, but that surely doesn't mean the absence of expectations for student performance in every school in those states. The real issue is whether those expectations are clear, open, and fair, or whether they are shrouded in mystery, and dependent upon using the bell curve to compare one student to another.

One experiment you can do right now is to ask a group of fourth-grade teachers to give advice to a mythical new third-grade teacher. "What should those third-grade students know and be able to do so that they can enter your fourth-grade classes with confidence and success?" I'm willing to bet that the fourth-grade teachers will have a remarkably thoughtful and focused set of advice to offer that third-grade teacher. It is human nature that it is easier to give advice than to take it. When the same group of fourth-grade teachers faces the question, "What will we give up?" (In other words, "What are we willing to stop teaching, in order to focus on the most important topics?"), the answer is likely to be, "Nothing." Moreover, there can be strikingly different opinions about what is most important.

You might also consider Larry Ainsworth's books *"Unwrapping" the Standards* and *Power Standards*—you don't need to wait for your state to develop standards to use the practical and helpful advice you'll find there.

We have been going through the process of identifying Power Standards in our K–5 math curriculum. We have used the accordion model to move information back and forth between a smaller subcommittee and each grade level at each elementary school. The committee and grade levels are satisfied with the standards we identified using the state's blueprint for test information. How can I explain why we haven't identified all of the standards? Our curriculum director is not familiar with the Power Standards

concept, and is fearful that the standards that have not been identified will not be taught. We are trying to reassure her. Is there anything that lists the "leftover" standards and explains how they are addressed when Power Standards are taught?

 I certainly understand the concern of your colleagues who think that teachers need to cover everything—after all, "it might be on the state test!" But the problem with that logic is that there is just no evidence that: a) Every standard can be covered in a 180-day school year; b) Every standard is of equal importance; and c) Teachers "covering" a subject is equivalent to students learning it. By contrast, there is substantial evidence that mastery of key Power Standards (see Larry Ainsworth's book *Power Standards*) helps students improve test performance and overall achievement.

Rather than trying to convince your colleagues, you can do some experiments to test the hypothesis of Power Standards. First, identify some of them in a specific grade and discipline—sixth-grade math, for example. Then get a copy of a sample assessment for that grade level, and count the number of items on the sample assessment that were addressed by the Power Standards. I did this once and found that the sixth-grade Power Standards addressed about 82 percent of the content on the test—not perfect, but not bad. So the question is, are we better off with students who have mastered 82 percent of the content of the test, or are we better off with students who have been exposed to 100 percent of the test, but have perhaps mastered only 40–50 percent of the content?

See Robert J. Marzano and John S. Kendall's work on this. It's just not a reasonable conclusion to claim that it's possible to for teachers to cover (and for students to master) every standard.

 In our state, where we have begun using standards-based education relatively recently, one issue has become a sticking point for some of our schools. What are your thoughts about posting or displaying the actual standards in the classroom?

Our schools are all over the place with this issue. Some of our elementary teachers have wall-papered their rooms with all of the standards for the year. Some teachers display only the standards

they are currently using. Some of our secondary teachers want to use only essential questions. Many of our secondary schools are invested heavily in Max Thompson's Learning-Focused School Model.

From the Department of Education perspective, we are promoting the importance of the "communication of the standard" to the students. I, personally, don't believe that many of our teachers see the power of thoroughly explaining the standards to the students so that they can help with their own learning. One of my friends even suggested that standards should be posted to keep the teacher on track.

 I do understand the impulse to post standards, particularly when visiting administrators tend to look for the standards on the wall and, I hope, look even more carefully that teaching and learning in the classroom are related to the standards. However, I'd like to offer a suggestion that could address the reluctance of teachers who see posting standards as a meaningless display, and also the concerns of administrators who see the posting of standards as a necessary discipline. My suggestion is that teachers and students work together to post the standards in *student-accessible language* so that 1) there is intellectual energy invested in the process—not just the physical energy of taping paper to the wall; and 2) educators are certain that the postings have relevance to real learning, not just the intent of policy makers and administrators. One of the things that Robert Marzano (2009a) and many other researchers have established clearly is that students learn better when they understand their learning goals. My work has also suggested that learning goals and teacher feedback are only useful when students understand them.

Two examples illustrate the point. First, consider the "class rules" that many teachers post on the first day of school. The best teachers engage the students in creating these rules and express the rules in a way that every student in the class can understand and apply. Teachers do this because they regard discipline, safety, and respect as essential norms for an effective classroom, and know that norms are only successful when every member of the community—not just the teacher—reinforces them. Second, consider playground games. Listen to students explain the rules to other students. "You can go here, but you can't go there; you can do this, but you can't do that." They are exceptionally precise, and the newest student in class can quickly learn to play the game.

CHAPTER 2

Instruction

Instruction

At my high school, we are questioning the order in which we teach math subjects. We teach Algebra, then Geometry, then Algebra 2. I was taught Algebra 2 before Geometry. Is one more conducive to student learning than the other?

I would recommend a new strategy being used by some schools: Integrated Algebra and Geometry—a two-year course that includes both subjects. A great deal of algebra instruction benefits from illustration with geometric concepts.

Another part of the faculty to include in this discussion is your science teachers. Many of them have told me that they have saved a great deal of time, and made their content more accessible to students, when they coordinated with their colleagues in math so that the math essential for physics, chemistry, and biology preceded the science instruction.

I am an eleven-year teacher of high school Italian and an extracurricular activity advisor for a community service after-school group. I love teaching Italian, and my mandate is to achieve results on the New York State Regents standardized test, which I have managed to do relatively well. Nevertheless, I always find it a chore to convince kids of the intrinsic value of education. It is hard to find, for each student, the reason each discipline is important—including Italian.

I am looking for ways to weave the relevance of the Italian language into community service activities and service-learning; these are potential ways to make this language and culture more meaningful to the students. When I was in school, I thought that being able to read, analyze, or feel a work of art or literature was, in and of itself, gratifying and enriching. Now, it seems that the thrill of learning is much more difficult to evoke or stimulate. Do you have any suggestions to share?

A My initial reaction to your question about the value of Italian to today's students includes the following: fortissimo, forte, piano, pianissimo.

Students respond to music partly because music expresses what words do not express. What they may not know is that Italian, among all languages, links together composers and listeners from many different cultures, countries, and languages. Austrians and Africans, Germans and Chinese, French and Russians, all use the Italian language to find common ground when they talk about music. They don't say "fast"; they say "allegro." And they don't say "very slow"; rather, they say "largo." They don't say "slow down"; they say "ritardando."

Students appreciate multi-cultural communication and they *love* criticism of and indignation about a single monolithic culture. Teachers can channel that indignation into a love of exploration and learning. You can take any genre of music—rap, baroque, romantic, or rock 'n roll, and find common ground in the Italian notation of emotion, speed, and volume. "Rubato"—if that is not the definition of adolescent creativity, I don't know what is.

Q 13 Middle school is a critical transition period between elementary school, where students get a lot of hands-on attention from teachers, and high school, where teachers present the material and students are responsible for their own learning.

What can I do to help students who haven't built the skills necessary to be independent learners, especially students with disabilities, Individualized Educational Program (IEP) students, and students whose emotional needs hinder their ability to gain the skills to be successful?

 A The challenge of building independent learning skills is certainly not limited to students with IEPs or emotional disabilities. Many students, including those with very high intelligence, have difficulty with the organizational, teamwork, project-management, and time-management skills required for success in school.

One technique I have used with students is the "menu" system for assignments and assessments. It allows the teacher to build these skills, differentiate instruction, and maintain an ethical standard in which the teacher expects the same standard of work from every student.

In the menu system, every student must accumulate 900 points for an "A" and 800 points for a "B." I won't negotiate for a lower grade. Some students who already have successful independent work skills might tackle a complex 200-point project. Other students, who lack those skills, and who need a great deal more incremental feedback from me, might take on eight separate 25-point projects to receive the same number of points. The quantity and quality of the work will be the same. I'm not "giving a break" to the second group of students who are doing 25-point projects, but rather helping them understand the building blocks of planning, organizing, and executing successful large projects. When a student "fails," then the consequence is not failure, but rather identifying what went wrong, selecting something else from the menu, taking personal responsibility, and *doing the work*. Some students simply give up in the face of overwhelming assignments, or they put them off until the last minute and guarantee failure. Teachers simply do not have time to give incremental feedback to 150 students. But this differentiated approach allows me to be fair and effective. I'm not saying it's 100 percent effective, but it is much, much better than the alternative of "one-size-fits-all," with the same assignments for students who bring to the classroom a wide range of preparation, background, and readiness.

We are currently at a crossroads in the development of curriculum and the adoption of textbooks in our district. Historically, the schools in our district have each been allowed to develop their own curriculum guides and adopt their own textbooks, without any connectivity or commonality between schools. Our assistant superintendent is attempting to rein in our school sites and is developing common curriculum and adopting common textbooks within and across school sites in our district, the purpose being to provide commonality and connectivity. I am a curriculum auditor with Curriculum Management Systems, Inc. and have researched the work of Dr. Fenwick English relative to this issue, but I am also very interested in your take on the issue of common curriculum and common textbooks within a school district.

A First, common curriculum without common formative assessments is a waste of time—an illusion that allows the central office to display nice documents to outside inspectors, but which does not have a real impact on the classroom. Perhaps that sounds a bit harsh, but I've seen too much money and time wasted on an "aligned curriculum" that is nothing more than a conversation (and lots and lots of three-ring binders) among a few people. If it doesn't have a practical, specific, and measureable impact on the classroom, then having a common curriculum is worthless. I'm sure that you've seen some of this in your work as a curriculum auditor. Unfortunately, the reaction to many such audits is the production of more documents at the central office, rather than meaningful changes at the school and classroom levels.

Second, we must acknowledge that the needs of different schools and classrooms really are *different*. I'm always amused when central offices insist on pacing guides, alignment, and consistency—right after they made educators sit through a lecture about the virtues of differentiation. Leaders must be clear about where there should be consistency (high expectations, Power Standards, core content) and where there should be variation that is not only permitted, but celebrated. Teachers and principals feel sucker-punched each time the pendulum swings from one extreme to the other.

In sum, this goes to issues far deeper than textbook adoption. I would ask the defenders of choice, "Are you willing to allow each school to have so much latitude in its selection of textbooks and curriculum that it can systematically have lower expectations of students based on the personal preferences of faculty and administrators?" I would ask the defenders of consistency, "Are you willing to admit that if a student is three years behind in reading, but we expect that student to graduate from high school some day, then we will need different curricula, assessments, and teaching practices for that student this year?"

Q 15 **Do you have any research relating to academic achievement and GPA eligibility requirements for sports?**

Thanks very much for your inquiry. This is an interesting "chicken and egg" question: "Do kids do better in school because they want to be in sports?" If so, then academic eligibility requirements might be a good incentive. Or, on the other hand, do kids who are in sports do better in school because of higher engagement, motivation, discipline, and relationships with coaches? If so, then academic eligibility requirements are backwards—rather than taking kids out of sports who are doing poorly in school, we should be putting more and more kids *into* sports, so that they will then do better in school.

The research on the subject is pretty conclusive that the second method is better. A synthesis of the research (Black, 2002; Fredricks & Eccles, 2006; Fujita, 2006; Holloway, 2002) shows that kids in sports and other extracurricular activities had better achievement, behavior, and engagement than kids not in extracurricular activities. In fact, when they studied the *same kids* during and outside of their sport's season, they performed better academically in season. I've also seen high-performing schools creating goals to have *every* student, including low-performing students, involved in at least one extracurricular activity, believing that the appropriate kind of peer pressure (Hey—you have to come to school—we *need* you) is more effective than adult pressure, and leads to improved attendance, behavior, and achievement.

 Do you have some references or data about students who are placed in combination classes? I am the principal of a school with a 20:1 ratio in the primary grades, so school enrollment often necessitates combining classes. Parents may better accept the idea if there is some information I could share that would allay their fears that their child isn't going to receive a good experience in such a setting. Clearly, qualified, enthusiastic teachers do make a difference, but research could be useful in enrolling parent support.

 I have the following observations for you:
1. Teacher quality is the most important variable in influencing student instruction; more important than class size, grade configuration, brand name, building label—you name it. It's all about the quality of the teachers and building leaders.

2. When the "20:1" rule is employed too strictly, so that anyone with a normal body temperature and clean fingerprints can be a teacher, the practical result is that poor children can have many years of unqualified teachers in the classroom. Small class size with unqualified teachers is a recipe for disaster. See the article "College Access, K–12 Concentrated Disadvantage, and the Next 25 Years of Education Research" by John T. Yun and José F. Moreno in *Educational Researcher* (2006) for definitive evidence on this point.

3. Combined classes present opportunities and challenges. The opportunity is that the advanced third grader can learn with the fourth graders, and the challenged fourth grader can have comfort and success with the third grade material. The challenge is that teachers, being human, are already being burned to a cinder preparing for one grade level. Preparing for multiple grade levels requires super-human effort, and is probably not sustainable. However, if I had to choose between a combined class with a qualified teacher, or distinct grade-level classes with an unqualified teacher, I would take the former any day of the week.

 Our staff is trying to make an informed decision about traditional spelling programs. Is there research indicating a relationship between spelling programs and increased achievement?

 I honestly do not know the answer to this question, and I'm a fairly voracious consumer of research. Therefore, you might consider another approach—action research. Consider asking teachers to engage in explicitly different strategies. One group of teachers engages in direct instruction in spelling (and perhaps other conventions), along with writing assignments; the other group focuses on writing assignments without this direct instruction. Both groups produce work products, such as stories or essays, to be evaluated (student identity anonymous, of course) by independent reviewers.

What do the results suggest to you and your faculty? What's the worst that can happen? Either way, teachers are encouraging more writing and students are doing more writing. Either way, students will eventually need to improve spelling and conventions.

My book *Reframing Teacher Leadership to Improve Your School* explains how this action research approach will lead to better buy-in for any reform within your school and district.

 I want to improve the learning capability of my children. I am especially worried about my younger son, who is eleven years old. He is not taking an interest in his education. He is in fourth grade, and this year he is failing. He tries to learn his books and work, but he forgets his lessons. Please give me advice about what procedures we can adopt to improve his learning and help him pass his exams, because his age group is advancing to the next grade level, and his younger brother is also advancing to the next grade level.

 First, identify what your son *does* find interesting. Does he like cricket, football, or electronic games? Use these interests as leverage to turn him back to studies. For example, if he needs to improve his writing, have him write a persuasive essay explaining the reasons that one team is superior to another, or why one electronic game is more sophisticated than another. Nonfiction writing—persuasion, description, and analysis—is a key to improved student achievement. Writing is best described as "thinking through the end of a pen" (King, 2002). The more that your son writes, the better his analysis, thinking, and reasoning will become. He is most likely to write more when he writes about subjects in which he has an interest. Right now, he probably sees academic work as completely separate from what he loves to do. You can help him see that academic work is *part* of what he loves to do. If he is studying English, you might want to consider English-language magazines that will spark his interest, such as "Sports Illustrated Kids," or similar magazines that are designed for young people.

Second, it is very important that your son think through and talk about his failure this past year. If he says, "I am a failure," then he is very likely to repeat the same mistakes. What he needs to think is, "I made some bad decisions last year, but I can make different decisions next year. I am not a failure. I am a smart boy and I can make better decisions next year." Then you and he can work together this summer to prove to yourselves and to his teachers that he is not a failure, that he is intelligent and capable, and that he has the ability to succeed. You might even ask him to show his teacher some of the essays that he writes about sports and games. Those essays should, of course, be excellent work, with superior vocabulary, composition, and organization.

Third, have a conversation with your son's teachers or school leaders. The focus of the conversation should be inquiry, not argument. The only relevant questions are, "What do you recommend that my son do in order to improve?" and "Is there anything my son can do *right now* in order to make up work and improve his scores?"

I find in many cases that failure is not due to a lack of intellectual ability, but rather poor organization and time management. Students—particularly boys who are eleven to fourteen years of age—need intensive help to get organized. I required that my son keep an assignment calendar and review it every day. When he said, "I've finished all my homework," I could look at the calendar and say, "Yes—but you have a test in two days, so you must study for that before you say that you have everything completed." This does not always work. Sometimes he completed homework, but he failed to submit it. Therefore, I am not telling you that I have all the answers or that I am a perfect parent. But I think these suggestions might help put your son on the path to success.

Q 19 **Have you looked at or collected any data related to the impact of single-gender education? Have any of the schools or classrooms that you studied been single-gender?**

A I recently attended a research conference where this subject was addressed. The findings of the Clark County, Nevada researchers were not unusual: single-gender classrooms work for some kids, but not for others (www.inform.com). Specifically, they found that girls usually had greater class participation, achievement, and engagement in single-gender classrooms.

Middle school boys in single-gender classrooms, on the other hand, continued to engage in behavior that was disruptive, competitive, and designed to show off their prowess, however irrelevant it might be the subject at hand. I propose that there is a clinical diagnosis for such a condition among middle school boys—it's called *normal.*

What I particularly appreciated about the Clark County researchers is that they did not gravitate to either of the political extremes in this debate—"single-gender is evil" or "single-gender is perfect"—but rather took a nuanced approach, concluding that sometimes it works and sometimes it doesn't.

Given ambiguous results, what is the best public policy? It seems to me that educators and school leaders should listen to two primary resources—evidence and kids. Evidence says that girls in particular will participate more when they are not in an environment in which they equate being pretty with being dumb. So let them have math, science, physical education, and health alone. Also listen to the kids. For all their bravado about their emerging sexuality, they are in reality quite modest, and deeply resent things like mixed physical education classes. Listen to the kids when they say, "Leave us *alone.*" They may not want to admit it, but the kids of today are not so sure that their "peace and free love and let it all hang out" teachers of the past 30 years were so smart in these matters. I realize that I'm sounding terribly old-fashioned, so I suggest that you don't listen to me, but rather listen in a systematic, non-threatening, and confidential way to your own students.

Scholars have noted some cultural differences surrounding gender to which we should pay attention. If there is a Latina who will not ask a male teacher for a homework extension because of a sick niece, nephew, or child, then we're not going to fix that with cultural awareness training. We need a system that allows this young woman to get help, not excuses, and that allows the teacher to focus on results, not compliance. Let's stop the "one-size-fits-all" regimen of homework and tests, and instead focus on genuine academic achievement.

Our school is in flux, and the new administration is designing a block schedule, with 45 minutes designated for language arts for grades 4–6. My question relates to the timing for language instruction. The fourth grade is scheduled to learn language arts at the end of the day. As a teacher trained in elementary education, I've always believed that language instruction is so

intense that it should be done when children are least tired and more likely to understand the concepts and skills. Is there any research on this issue?

 There are several ways to avoid the "end-of-the-day fatigue" syndrome that you are concerned about. One is to move language arts closer to the beginning of the day, and another is to rotate all subjects, as many schools do. But your letter raises a much more important point than "morning" or "afternoon," and that is the amount of time devoted to language arts. In my view, 45 minutes is woefully inadequate for reading and writing instruction at *any* grade, but particularly in the grades that you mentioned. Unless you have student achievement data that conclusively shows that 100 percent of your students are at or above grade level in reading and writing, please reconsider this schedule.

In my judgment, 90 minutes per day of language arts instruction is a minimum, and for students who are under-performing, you may want to consider allowing even more time. *The Journal of Educational Psychology* (Capella & Weinstein, 2001) reported that eighth-grade students who are not reading on grade level have an 85 percent probability of remaining below grade level throughout all of high school. Whatever else you do in grades 4–8, please get 100 percent of students reading and writing at grade level.

 I am hearing more and more teachers complaining about lack of student motivation. Do any of your materials identify ways to assist teachers in motivating kids for success?

The general factors associated with student motivation are:

Choice: Consider using homework menus, offering a choice of 25 out of 30 items on tests, and offering a choice of prompts in writing. When students choose, they are making a bet that they know more than the teacher; that they are making a good choice that gives them the best chance of success, and thus they tend to produce results that are self-fulfilling prophecies.

Power: Have students write test questions, prompts, and rubrics. The results tend to be rigorous and clear.

Efficacy: Give students the sense that hard work (not luck or innate ability) yields better results, and that, therefore, *any* student can succeed. Teachers should be very clear in how they give feedback, not praising "effortless brilliance," but hard work that yields results.

Competence: Engender in students a sense of competence—the biggest motivator of all. The same "unmotivated" kids who won't do anything in class will remain engaged in other activities (video games, basketball, hockey) for hours on end because they believe that their hard work pays off. The central question for teachers is "How can I provide my students with feedback that has the immediacy, clarity, and precision that a video game offers? How can I make my students want to 'get to the next level' as they do in that game?" I don't have all the answers, but I have learned that immediate feedback (not next day or next week, but within minutes or even seconds), is what students really value, whether it's an essay or an advanced statistics problem.

 How can I facilitate a conversation among teachers to identify their key eight to ten big ideas per course when their shared knowledge of each topic is all across the board? We need to identify the "refrigerator curriculum," not only for parent communication, but also, and most importantly, to focus teaching efforts to increase student achievement. What kind of time should we allow for this conversation? Do you recommend a vertical meeting first, or not until after each grade level/department has identified its essential standards?

 One resource that will be particularly helpful for this discussion is *Power Standards* by Larry Ainsworth. It will help you and your colleagues identify the most important standards, and focus on the issues that will provide the greatest benefit to your students.

Essentially, *Power Standards* will request that you consider three questions. First, "What endures?" Some standards require only transitory knowledge, while others require skills and knowledge that will endure throughout high school and college. Second, "What has leverage?" Some standards (graphs, nonfiction writing, reading) apply to many other standards—they have leverage—while other standards are more isolated. Third, and most importantly, "What is most essential for the next level of instruction?"

Your question said that your faculty was "all across the board," but I bet that if you ask them to give advice to the next lower grade level on what students need to know and be able to do in order to enter their class, you would find an astonishing level of consistency. When you ask teachers, "What will you give up?"—in other words, "What will you stop teaching, in order to focus on the most important topics?"—the answer is "Nothing!" But when you ask the same teachers to give advice to their peers in the next lower grade, then they provide a clear prescription for what is important that is brief, clear, and focused.

 You mentioned several researchers (Linda Darling-Hammond, John Goodlad, Michael Schmoker and yourself) when stating that teacher effectiveness is the key variable for influencing achievement and equity. I would be interested in reading that research. Can you tell me what journal articles or books have been written about this topic?

 These are all very prolific authors, so I'll just mention a few highlights.

- Linda Darling-Hammond's classic is *The Right to Learn*, but she has written many good books and articles. One recent article, "The Flat Earth and Education: How America's Commitment to Equity will Determine Our Future," was published in *Educational Researcher* in August 2007. You might also want to check out her Stanford University Web page.

- John Goodlad is similarly exceptional, but his classic is *A Place Called School* (1984).

- Michael Schmoker's most recent book is *Results Now* (2006), but I would also look at *The Results Fieldbook* (2001).

- I've written more than twenty books, so I'll try to narrow the focus. The issue of teaching effectiveness is addressed in *Accountability for Learning* and *The Learning Leader*. There are also many free downloads and articles about the subject on the Leadership and Learning Center Web site, www.LeadandLearn.com.

We are working very hard with our teacher teams on having focused conversations about student work. What are some key questions that teams should be asking? Are there certain things that you have discovered that effective teams do?

You might want to look at Richard DuFour's work on this issue, as well as that of Robert Marzano and Larry Ainsworth. I'd focus on questions such as, "What is most important for students to learn?" (see Ainsworth's *Power Standards*) and "What will we do if students are not successful?"

I am looking for an article or some type of literature that addresses standards-based instruction. More specifically, I am looking for anything that has been written that focuses on the conflict that teachers may face when the standards tell them they should be teaching a specific concept at a specific time of year, but the assessments they are administering in their classrooms are telling them something different. For example, based on their skill level, students may not be ready for the concepts that the standard specifies should be taught at a particular time.

The best source on this subject is *Power Standards* by Larry Ainsworth. As you quite correctly note, there is sometimes a conflict between the official curriculum and what some students need. If for example, it is Monday, and the pacing guide says that I must teach the Pythagorean Theorem on Tuesday, but my students need help with multiplication, exponents, and even the definition of a right triangle, then I'll probably need more than a day to get that done. I'm not suggesting dumbing down the curriculum—only acknowledging what every teacher knows: that there is a sequence to understanding, and that sometimes concepts take more time to teach and learn than a curriculum guide allows.

The reason that Power Standards are so important is that if I need to have that extra time to reinforce number operations and basic geometry, then I probably have to give up something else. My nominee for that distinction would be the rhombus, along with other things in the curriculum that don't help kids in their next year of study. This requires determination and surgical precision: "We're *not* going to do *this*, in order to have more time to do *that*."

In fact, teachers make these sorts of decisions all the time, but we do so in a personal, private, and idiosyncratic way. *Power Standards* helps us do so in a systematic and constructive way.

I am the principal of a K–4 elementary school. My staff is doing a very good job implementing Professional Learning Communities with Power Standards and data-based decision-making. The biggest barrier I hear is that the scope and sequence of the program doesn't allow them to stop and differentiate instruction. The analogy that I think fits this situation is that the teachers are on the train of teaching "the program," while many of the students are left at the depot.

I hear from many sources that we must remain true to the program (Open Court for reading, Investigations for math, etc.). But, when teachers do this, it causes them to go too fast and cover too much. The result is that the students are not learning as much.

To go with one of your points, learning should be the constant, and teaching and time should be the variables—it seems that we should modify the scope and sequence to ensure learning, not coverage.

It's not an either/or proposition—either we have the curriculum (Open Court or *any* curriculum—it's not the brand that makes that much difference) or we differentiate. The either/or premise is only true if, as you suggest, time is fixed. Take Open Court as an example—people argue vehemently over whether it works, but some schools give 60 minutes to the literacy block, while others give 90, 120, or 180 minutes. Those that give 180 minutes, not surprisingly, can both differentiate instruction and also meet their curriculum objectives.

Since 2004, I've documented time as a critical variable, yet I routinely hear that people believe the vendor myths that schools can accomplish all that they want, irrespective of student needs, without making fundamental changes in the schedule. It's just not true. Not every subject deserves the same amount of time, and not every subject needs to be taught every day. If we don't get literacy right, then nothing else matters. I know that statement drives crazy those who think that I am disrespecting social studies or that I'm just not clever enough to "read across the curriculum." But the plain truth is that covering social studies, science, or anything else is a meaningless exercise if kids can't read and write at grade level. This means giving them the time that they need, and for the other subjects, narrowing the focus to Power Standards and giving up the illusion of universal coverage.

As an elementary music teacher, I feel that I have a lot to offer, and that I am able to participate in our grade-level data teams. But I also struggle, because I am not able to be on a team of music educators that teach the same concepts and information. My thought is that if our music classes could improve instructionally and be more data-driven, it would also improve the overall education at our school. I can also see the value in everyone teaching reading and literacy, and I have long thought that should be happening. But I wonder if the best way for us to do that is for music teachers to actively look at our standards and figure out how we can best incorporate reading into our limited time. From time to time, we would certainly need to involve teachers that are experts in teaching reading, but I wonder if the timing could be decided better through an elementary music teacher data team.

I would appreciate your thoughts. What do you suggest? Continue with a grade-level data team? Form an elementary music team? Something else?

I don't know enough about your particular situation to suggest whether grade-level or multi-grade-level participation is best, but in general, my suggestion is that music teachers have so much to contribute that the broader your influence, the better. Think of your best professional development experiences that involved music. We didn't say, "That's only elementary," or "That's exclusively secondary," or even "That's only graduate school," but rather recognized the value of music at every level. My hope would be that schools would think of the very broad contributions music makes and integrate music with academics at every level, from teaching kindergarten songs that reinforce memory to encouraging seemingly non-musical high school students to write classical fugues and create rap lyrics.

I fear that this response doesn't give you a definitive answer, but when it comes to the role of music, I think that the most reliable answer is "yes"—and then let the music speak for itself.

 How can we teach kids attributes such as confidence, urgency, versatility, common sense, critical thinking, and team work?

 Teachers and school leaders can create these expectations in every task, assessment, project, and service learning opportunity that we provide. I don't think that teachers should have a "confidence, urgency…" lesson—rather, teachers should inculcate these characteristics into student performance at every level. For example:

Confidence: Teachers generate this best when they assign students work that challenges them. The student moves from "You've got to be kidding!" to "This teacher helped me do things that I never thought I could do." Great coaches do this regularly, as do music teachers. There is no reason we can't do the same thing in other classes. The key is feedback that is designed to improve performance rather than feedback that confirms students' belief that they are incapable.

Urgency: I believe in creating *immediate* consequences and *immediate* rewards. Miss an assignment? Don't give me an excuse; get it done *now*. Not prepared for class? Don't sit there and stare, get the books, pencils, paper, and anything else you need ready *now*. Come to class with homework done for the entire week and be ready for more advanced, challenging, and creative work. Here is a psychic reward—an opportunity for freedom, creativity, independence—right *now*.

Teamwork: Teachers can foster teamwork by letting students know that they are expected to take ownership of group projects. If a student is mad at a classmate for not pulling his or her weight on a project, get the complaining student to tell you how he or she plans to address the issue. Make it clear that you will be happy to watch the interaction and to support the student, but that you want him or her to take personal responsibility for making the team more effective.

I have a biology teacher who plans a field trip every year to a salmon hatchery. While I do not think there are any Power Standards that relate to this favorite activity, it seems reasonable that we could construct a standards rationale to justify the trip. How can I prompt her to think about a standards-based justification for this trip?

Field trips can certainly be consistent with Power Standards. Nonfiction writing is clearly a Power Standard, so I would hope that students are writing descriptive essays about what they saw. In addition, there must certainly be biology Power Standards about life cycles that can be taught in conjunction with this field trip. The real test of this, or any, activity is not "Is it popular?" but "Is it effective?" —that is, does it help students meet their learning objectives? Trips to the salmon hatchery, art museum, and symphony can all meet this requirement, provided the teacher is clear about what student learning activities will happen before, during, and after the trip. Where I teach, in order to justify time away from school, teachers need to prove that any time away from classes will help students in research, writing, speaking, and other core skills. That seems like a reasonable requirement, and one that is well within reach.

Can you please clarify for me what you feel is the best and most efficient method to employ when undertaking the task of learning a new language?

There is little question that immersion is the best way to learn a new language. That is why the best language teachers speak only the target language during class, use *lots* of visual stimuli so that students can associate new vocabulary with vivid visual images, and have immediate practice in speaking, writing, and formal and informal conversation, so that emotional barriers are reduced, student confidence is increased, and the language is the primary mode of communication.

The same is true in the "languages" of music and mathematics. Great teachers in those subjects use the language of music and the language of math to communicate. The music teacher does not just say "pianissimo," but whispers it in a barely audible voice, plays an instrument with exquisite gentleness, and then, to make the point, plays a crashingly loud chord and says "fortissimo!" followed by a return to "pianissimo" and whispers.

It's a long process, but teachers in all of these disciplines—language, music, and math—employ the same sort of techniques.

 Can you please provide me with more information about peer tutoring and its effectiveness?

 There are many sources on this; here are a few of them:

- *Show Me the Evidence!* by Robert Slavin and Olatokunbo Fashola makes the research case for cooperative learning.
- The June 2000 issue of *Harvard Education Letter* is devoted to different models of student cooperation and collaboration.
- *The Art of Teaching Writing* by Lucy Calkins includes many examples of student-to-student feedback.

If you are expecting students to give meaningful feedback to one another, then I would consider these issues:

1. Rubrics must be *detailed* and *objective*—it is imperative that students give accurate tutoring and feedback, and that their feedback is not clouded by subjectivity or the identity of the student who is receiving the feedback.

2. Students must *practice* giving feedback, both in writing with anonymous pieces of student work and orally in a fishbowl setting in front of the class.

3. Find *models* of situations in which peer tutoring is already successful in your school. I'd start this search in physical education and music classes. Figure out how you can emulate those models that are already successful with your students, so the concept seems less alien to them.

Effective tutoring, coaching, and feedback are difficult challenges, even for experienced teachers. We should not expect students to master this without practice and clear direction.

I work in a college preparatory charter high school. This will be our first year using a block schedule pattern. This is also my first year as principal. Developing the master schedule and designing a block that fits is my charge. I really want to be successful. Traditionally, our scholars attended classes in a fifty-five minute blocks, with two lunch periods of thirty minutes each and seven classes per day. Could you forward me any research about the pros and cons of block scheduling and sample schedules?

The bottom line on the block schedule is this: It doesn't matter, at least with respect to academic achievement. There is some limited data that block scheduling reduces discipline problems, principally because there are fewer passing periods, and that is the time when many student confrontations occur.

The biggest issue with block scheduling is that teachers have fewer periods to cover the same material. Some teachers who are used to having 180 discrete periods during the year have trouble adapting to having only 90. Some teachers have a tendency to use a 90-minute block as 60 minutes of instruction and 30 minutes of study hall. Then, in April, teachers realize that they have only covered material through January, so the last two months of the year are characterized by frantic coverage.

Therefore, the most important thing that instructional leaders must do is to identify exactly how the current curriculum fits into the new schedule. Moreover, teachers need clear and explicit models of how to use a block. I have students up and working in different spaces at least every 20–30 minutes. Teachers who use a block for a 90-minute movie or lecture will find that their students aren't learning much.

I have been struggling with the issues of ability-grouping, student achievement, and school culture. My question to you is whether you can share any data, opinions, or guidance about ability-grouping and its impact on student achievement. To elaborate briefly, I am aware of a great deal of opinion supporting ability-grouping from the gifted and talented point of view. My concern

is whether there is any evidence to support the notion that this "race to place," as I refer to it, is in some ways detrimental to students, and, moreover, to school culture, as the "non-gifted" are also indirectly identified. I am also interested in learning about other researchers' views on this topic and the determination of whether tracking/ability grouping is truly a treatment-effect program, or, in contrast, a selection-effect program.

Finally, it is my observation that we create egocentric students through the gifted identification process, rather than instilling leadership, initiative, and self-determination in our talented students. The cultural product here may be that students become elitist in their thinking, and have more difficulty dealing with diversity in many forms at school and later in the workplace. Again, these notions that I have outlined are merely observational and certainly only represent my personal opinions and concerns. I am wondering if anyone else is interested in these issues and how they are related to standards within our schools, and whether or not there is data that can be used to examine this objectively.

 First, with regard to your request for research, I would consider two sources. The June 2000 issue of *Harvard Education Letter* was devoted to research and practice on flexible grouping. I would also visit www.ascd.org, and look at *Show Me the Evidence!* By Robert Slavin and Olatokunbo Fashola, specifically the parts about cooperative learning.

Second, with regard to gifted education, I strongly agree. My own children have been involved in these programs, and when I hear parents and teachers talk about the "special needs" of these students, I can't help but ask myself, "Doesn't every student in this district deserve the same thing?" Frankly, it is quite common for the parent groups for "gifted" students (i.e., gifted economically, with print-rich environments and attentive parents) to be politically active and connected, and to demand extra resources and attention for their children. Poor children rarely have comparably powerful advocates. While this is incendiary and not politically correct, I have frequently observed the same phenomenon among the advocates for special education students. Much of what is called "special" education is, in fact, just "good" education; and the accommodations and adaptations are thoughtful and appropriate, and could benefit many students, not just those identified for special services.

Third, you have nailed the diversity issue on the head. We systematically lie to ourselves and to our communities when we say we have a "diverse" school, and then segregate students as soon as they walk in the door. If you want evidence of this, just compare the composition of advanced placement classes to the composition of the student body. If the former has the same percentage of poor students as the latter, I'll buy dinner.

CHAPTER 3

Writing
and Reading

Writing and Reading

 I am working as a literacy staff-developer/trainer in an elementary school. Our superintendent wants our schools to do more in the area of nonfiction writing. We are familiar with the research you published in the article "High Performance in High Poverty Schools: 90/90/90 and Beyond," but I need some more information on any research you have. We are trying to follow the standards for our state. Currently the primary grades 1–3 only require narrative and descriptive writing, and in grades 2 and 3, the friendly letter. Upper grades have standards that specifically address nonfiction writing. I know that students need to write in all content areas. I completely agree with this push to have kids do more nonfiction writing, but I need more information to give my primary teachers to support nonfiction writing. They feel like they are on overload just trying to meet the writing standards they already have.

 I'm not saying that I expect all elementary students to do all genres of nonfiction writing. But I *am* saying that in most classrooms, the vast majority of elementary writing is focused on fiction, personal narrative, fantasy, and poetry. Therefore, when these students are challenged to describe, compare, analyze, and persuade, they are overwhelmed by those demands.

I understand your desire to stay within the framework of the state standards, and I agree. Nonfiction writing can help students achieve standards in science, social studies, and many other areas. It's not, in other words, an additional requirement, but simply an excellent mechanism for helping students and teachers to do what they would have been doing anyway.

Finally, I completely understand the "overload" problem. That's why teachers should be using Power Standards, not frantically covering every standard in the state code. I'd particularly recommend the book *Power Standards* by Larry Ainsworth. You might also find my books *Reason to Write* and *Reason to Write: Student Handbook* useful.

My school has taken a very serious approach to the implementation of nonfiction writing. Our students are learning the process of writing in conjunction with science and social studies, as a backdrop for content. The students' papers are graded several times throughout the trimester, and they are given a "cold prompt" at the end of each trimester. We are using the prompt writing as a gauge of student learning. The cold prompt writing is what our question is about. When students are given a cold prompt, should they be allowed to use materials (such as a dictionary, a thesaurus, or a pre-written organizer that contains vocabulary) during the writing process? Can you recommend any research that is available regarding this topic?

In general, I think students should be encouraged to use resources such as a dictionary and a thesaurus for writing assignments. However, it is also important to take into account the emotional needs of students when you are matching the practice writing assessment environment to the actual writing assessments that they will have later. If you expect a student to take a writing test with only a prompt and blank paper and no resources, then certainly it is only fair that the student have the opportunity to practice in that environment.

With regard to the use of pre-written organizers, I'm not sure that they are particularly helpful if we expect students to ultimately be able to create their own organizers in order to frame their ideas.

With regard to research, there is significant research on the link between nonfiction writing and student achievement. Also, a recent *Journal of Educational Psychology* article (Kiuhara, Graham, & Hawken, 2009) demonstrated that students who use graphic organizers (which they have created themselves) have significantly better scores on writing assignments than students who do not.

Moreover, Dr. Mel Levine's books (2002, 2003) include research that special education students are particularly helped by the use of graphic organizers, and that is consistent with my own research and that of Robert Marzano.

But why not do some research of your own? Do an experiment this semester by having one class use the writing tools you suggest above and another class not use them. Compare their class average writing scores now, and then make another comparison after four months of the experiment, and see what you can learn. This sort of local action research can have as much credibility with your colleagues as a published study that I conduct a thousand miles away.

 How often should students be engaged in nonfiction writing in order for it to be most effective?

 My honest answer? After every meal. I've never been in a school with "too much" nonfiction writing. Every class offers opportunities for thinking, therefore, every class offers students opportunities to write (think) about questions such as:

- How would you summarize what we have discussed in the past thirty minutes?

- How is what we read and talked about today (or played, or drew, or danced) similar to and different from what we did yesterday?

- Look carefully at the (tree, frog, flower, equation, tapestry, mold, historical document) and describe it in detail.

 Regarding nonfiction writing, how long should students be required to write?

For the rest of their lives. But that's probably not what you meant. I think this really is an opportunity for differentiation. I have some students that will get stuck after two or three minutes, and I have to have a conference with them; I have other students who can be left alone to outline and then write for twenty to thirty minutes.

Teachers can expand students' capacity for writing for longer periods of time by starting with a time limit of three minutes and gradually extending the time limit to five, ten, fifteen, and twenty minutes over a period of time.

In one of your seminars, you referred to a study that supported the use of writing in science journals and said that it led to improved scores on standardized tests. I would very much like to read this study and to share it with the principals and instructional leaders in my district.

 There are many sources on this topic. I recommend the following:

- *The Daily Disciplines of Leadership* by Douglas Reeves
- *Accountability in Action*, 2nd ed., by Douglas Reeves
- *The Art of Teaching Writing*, by Lucy Calkins
- *The Right to Learn*, by Linda Darling-Hammond
- *The Myth of Laziness*, by Mel Levine

There is also a great National Science Foundation Study that is precisely on point to the impact of writing on science achievement. The "Four-Year Study of Student Achievement Data" was published in 2000 by Michael Klentschy, Leslie Garrison, and Olga Maia Amaral.

I'm sure that there are many more sources, but this is a pretty good start. Suffice it to say that nonfiction writing, along with editing and rewriting, is one of the best ways to help students think, reason, analyze, and deliberate. It is, in Dr. Levine's words, "the largest orchestra a kid will conduct."

In other words, writing does not detract from science or any other subject, but contributes to it.

 At a conference I attended, you addressed the topic of using scribes for children who are having difficulties with the physical aspect of the writing process. I'd like to hear these thoughts again, particularly as they pertain to children in the first and second grade.

 I just spent my morning with some very, very reluctant student writers. I know that they were all full of ideas, but in the case of one seventh grade boy in particular, his inability to write legibly transformed an otherwise bright and creative kid into one who was sullen and silent.

I think the use of a scribe, or of computer transcription technology, can be part of the solution, particularly when students seem paralyzed when told to put their ideas down on paper. Because it is *so* motivating for students to see their ideas, words, and names in print, the earlier we can do that, the better. That said, we nevertheless have an obligation to get students to use pencil and paper to communicate, and with each year of delay, we are closer to having middle school students (the the ones with whom I worked this morning) who are facing multiple course failures because nobody can read their writing. Computers are not sufficient for many homework and in-class assignments that require writing, and these students are not eligible for special education services—they simply never have learned to write legibly.

When it comes to first- and second-grade students, I think you can have both—you can get the kids' ideas on paper (with the help of scribes or transcription software, if necessary) and also attend to the need of those students to develop the skills necessary for legibility. You can use the scribes or transcription software to accelerate the pace of students' thinking, writing, and gaining recognition and feedback. Then, as that feedback fires students' motivation, you can gradually require more student responsibility for writing. You might start by having the students just be responsible for the caption on a picture, then the caption and the title, then the caption, title, and lead sentence. I have worked in several schools this year, including high-poverty schools, where kindergarten students are writing three to four legible sentences by mid-year. When people say that it is not "developmentally appropriate" for five- and six-year-old children to hold a pencil and write legibly, that is a statement that kids don't believe, so I don't see why we should believe it, either.

 Is there a standard rubric that you can suggest that can be used for nonfiction writing across subject areas?

 Rubrics tend to vary depending on the subject, with some subjects, such as math, emphasizing only organization and conventions, and other subjects, such as English and history, emphasizing voice, vocabulary, and argumentation. You can find some really good ones at every grade level and every subject in the *Write to Know* series, available on The Leadership and Learning Center Web site, www.LeadandLearn.com.

 Should more emphasis be placed on the writing process, the curriculum content, or a combination of both?

 It really is a combination—process is *not enough* if students fail to learn the content. But content mastery is *not enough* if students cannot transform a bullet list of facts and ideas into a coherent series of sentences and paragraphs.

 I am a literacy coach who plans and facilitates professional development at an elementary school. As a staff, we have read and reviewed your article "High Performance in High Poverty Schools: 90/90/90 and Beyond." We then listed some of the things we are already doing to improve literacy and made a list of other ideas we thought we would pursue.

In the article, you mention that teachers in successful 90/90/90 schools "typically used a single scoring rubric to evaluate student writing and applied this scoring guide to every piece of written work." Some of us have worked with a variety of different rubrics in the past, for example, 6 + 1 Trait® Writing, Step Up to Writing®, Rubrics, Colorado Student Assessment Program (CSAP) rubrics, and classroom-made rubrics, so we are wondering what a "single scoring rubric" might look like. We are also interested in whether the rubrics were specific to primary grades, intermediate grades, each grade level or the whole school. Our staff thinks that they would like to develop a whole-school rubric to facilitate cross-grade-level conversations. Any clarification on this topic would be greatly appreciated.

 I *love* the idea of you creating your own rubric. If you want to have full buy-in, ownership, and commitment by teachers and students, then they should be the creators and owners of those documents.

Obviously, your rubrics should be at least as rigorous as those used by the state. My experience is that teacher-created (and even student-created) rubrics are clear, thoughtful and rigorous.

When I referred to all written work, I meant that the same simplified rubric can be used not only for English language arts classes, but also for science reports, social studies essays, and every other subject. Certainly there are higher levels of detail on some elements of voice and composition that an English teacher may use, but there ought to be a few things—organization, conventions, some basic elements of expression—that students *always* use in *every* class. It's somewhat like discipline—if we want our system to be effective, students need to know that the rules always apply, not that spelling and punctuation are only important in some classes, but not in others. As a math teacher, I'm not going to go crazy over semicolons, simile, metaphor, and irony—but I do insist that my math students write neatly, start with capital letters, end with appropriate punctuation, and organize their thoughts with a clear beginning, middle, and end. Dr. Mel Levine, author of *A Mind at a Time*, and I both insist that students write and speak in complete sentences in all classes.

 You stated during a recent presentation that reading scores are positively affected when teachers spend time teaching how to read nonfiction. The principal is requiring that we provide data that proves this before we can use certain materials we have purchased for our classroom. These materials require students to read a nonfiction passage, answer short response questions, use graphic organizers, and answer multiple choice questions. Can you forward any data that may assist us in these efforts?

 My research has supported not only nonfiction reading, but, most importantly, nonfiction *writing*. You'll see this published in many of my books, including *The Daily Disciplines of Leadership, Accountability for Learning*, and *The Learning Leader*. Essentially, nonfiction writing in higher amounts, along with collaborative scoring and multiple opportunities for student success (editing and rewriting), are all practices associated with better scores in literacy, math, science, and social studies.

But I want to offer a gentle challenge here—what if there were no research at all? Would that be a good reason *not* to do more reading and writing? I really trust teachers—I am one—and I think teachers' instincts are very sound. We know that when students work hard, respect our feedback, and focus on developing their minds, they do better in a variety of subjects.

Do you know if a study has been done comparing reading nonfiction to reading fiction, with regard to its impact on student achievement and learning? Any insights would be appreciated.

First, it's not just a fiction vs. nonfiction dichotomy when it comes to reading. There is substantial evidence that student choice is related to higher levels of engagement, but that "choice" could be anything from a book about Harry Potter to a book about how to get rich. In other words, it's not just the genre, but the thought process behind the selection of the book that is important.

Second, consider the vocabulary, complexity, and challenge. Although I'm a fan of nonfiction literature, I can't endorse the dumbed down "nonfiction lite" that is often offered to students over novels and fantasy that are rich in content and complexity.

Finally, before you look for outside research, consider creating your own action research projects so that teachers and colleagues will engage in inquiry, experiments, research, and findings that will be far more credible than anything that I or other outsiders can provide.

What is your opinion on scripted reading programs and assessments, such as Open Court, DIBELS, Corrective Reading, Success for All, etc.? As an educator of 29 years, I've seen the pendulum swing back and forth. I experienced Corrective Reading first-hand years ago and was not at all impressed. I've done some research, and read much of Gerald Coles' book *Reading the Naked Truth: Literacy, Legislation, and Lies,* and I'm also reading Elaine Garan's work in *Resisting Reading Mandates*. Since there is talk of purchasing a reading program, such as Open Court, in our district, I am concerned that I may have to be an unpopular voice in speaking out against programs that I believe are not in the best

interests of our students.

What types of reading programs were in place in schools such as the ones in your 90/90/90 studies and in other schools experiencing noteworthy success? Our district is an inner-city school district, with a high minority population.

From the research that I have done, I am concerned that these types of scripted reading programs are a quick fix targeted at low-performing inner city student populations. They do not seem conducive to your *Making Standards Work* model. What do you think?

 I recently wrote a column for *Education Gadfly* (Reeves, 2006) that is directly on point to this matter. Here is the short version of that column: It's not the brand name; it's you. In other words, you can always find conflicting research on each of the programs that you listed—It works! No, it's awful! No, it works! Who is right? Neither, if they are only examining the presence or absence of a program. The relevant variables are, as you suggest, the teaching and leadership. There are times when direct instruction or other scripted techniques can be effective, but only when accompanied by thoughtful teaching, leadership, and other supporting contexts. The same programs can be utterly ineffective without the necessary context. I don't think that the research supports either an endorsement or an indictment of scripted reading programs. It's the contextual variables—most importantly the quality of classroom teaching—that are far more important.

 What are your thoughts on the Reading Recovery® program? We have a strong camp of Reading Recovery® teachers in our district, but I find they are not willing to look at the child and his or her needs, but rather want to perform the requirements of the program. Therefore, they feel that kids who are not "fixed" after Reading Recovery® need special education services. It is such an expensive program, and our data is not reflecting that this program is having a dramatic long-term effect on our kids.

 I think this is being cast as an "either/or" proposition—either Reading Recovery® or special education, and that's not what the research supports. According to John Hattie in *Visible Learning* (2009, p. 140), Reading Recovery® is most effective when it is a supplement to, not a substitute for, classroom teaching. He cited other studies that concluded that "well-designed, reliably implemented, one-to-one interventions can make a significant contribution to improved reading outcomes for many students whose poor reading skills place them at risk of academic failure."

He says that "Reading Recovery® is a second-chance program undertaken over a twelve to twenty week specified period. Children are discontinued from the program *when it is agreed that they are ready to return to regular classroom instruction*" (emphasis added, p. 138).

Hattie further emphasizes "the five pillars of good reading instruction: phonemic awareness, phonics, fluency, vocabulary, and comprehension—and attending to all is far more critical than whether the program teaches one of the five as opposed to another. The most effective programs for teaching reading first attend to the visual and auditory perceptual skills. Then a combination of vocabulary, comprehension, and phonics instruction with repeated reading opportunities is the most powerful set of instructional methods. The least effective methods are whole language, sentence combining, and assuming that students will learn vocabulary incidentally when reading. If reading is not successful the first time, then second-chance programs such as Reading Recovery® are most effective."

You might have some students who receive the program for twelve weeks, and others for twenty weeks, but the later you reach them, the more intensive the intervention will have to be and the longer it will take. In the 90/90/90 schools, they spend 180 minutes *every day* on literacy instruction. If a child spent seven, eight, or nine years digging a literacy hole, he or she won't dig out in 90 minutes a day. Moreover, when students are "pulled out" for extra literacy, they should *not* be *pulled out of literacy*—they need both regular instruction *and* intervention.

This is one of those areas where the research is so clear it is difficult to equivocate, or to let people impose personal beliefs over evidence.

When Reading Recovery® is done well, as described above, the effect size (proportion of a standard deviation) of improvement in student achievement is, according to Hattie's meta-meta-analysis, .96. That is more than twice the size of a "significant" effect size (.40) and greater than that of both student socioeconomic status (.57) and parent involvement (.51). In sum, Reading Recovery® is the right thing to do, but you've got to do it right.

CHAPTER 4

Assessments

Assessments

My administration has started our school down the road toward implementing common assessments. This seems to be a very effective way to ensure equal and fair learning opportunities for all students. Unfortunately, as with most other ideas, the teachers of electives (technology, foreign languages, art, music, consumer science, study hall, etc.) are placed into a "discipline team" together and asked to participate in the common assessment strategy. Is this a fair application of this strategy? Can teachers of electives create a common assessment across our different curricula? Or, should we spend the time finding other ways to promote reading, writing, and math literacy in our content areas?

I can see validity on both sides of this. I have seen some terrific writing assessments in music and art, and I would hate to have those efforts diluted. On the other hand, in many school systems, the student-to-teacher ratio for music, art, and physical education is *much* higher than for other classes, and the use of common assessments can place an excessive burden on those teachers compared to their colleagues. Some team assessment might make sense—have students study Igor Stravinsky's *Firebird Suite* in music class and artistic representations of it in art class, and submit written reflection for credit in both classes, with grading duties split between the two teachers.

At the end of the day, we need to honor your desire to focus on your discipline and use your expertise to help students link literacy skills to your class, without drowning you in paperwork. There must be a reasonable compromise here somewhere—perhaps one quarter doing discipline-specific assessments and the next quarter doing cross-disciplinary assessments.

What is your opinion on how frequently benchmark assessments should be given? We have been told to test every three weeks and the teachers feel they don't have enough time left for instruction.

A I'm an advocate of very short (ten- to twelve-item) assessments done very frequently. In my classes, I would do weekly assessments, but many schools are doing biweekly assessments successfully. Certainly formative assessments must be no less frequent than quarterly.

The key is not, however, simply "doing" the assessment—the key is how teachers use the results to make immediate improvements in teaching and learning. The longer the interval between the assessments, the less likely it is that teachers can make meaningful alterations in teaching strategies and curriculum.

With regard to the "not enough time for instruction" argument, I can only quote what I heard another Virginia educator say when confronted with the same challenge. "These (biweekly) assessments *save* us time—it's the only way we know what to teach and who needs special assistance."

There is not a shred of evidence that covering the curriculum and checking off items on pacing charts is equivalent to student learning. In areas where students succeed—from electronic games to music to athletics—they receive very frequent feedback. Robert Marzano is just one of many researchers who has established that of all the things that we do as teachers, feedback has the single greatest influence on student achievement, provided that the feedback is timely, accurate, and specific. End-of-semester final exams do not meet any of those criteria.

I am very sympathetic to teachers who feel overwhelmed by the sheer quantity of standards and curriculum elements. The best response to that challenge, however, is not a failure to assess students, but rather a narrowing of the scope of the assessments. It is not necessary to address every element of the standards. Teachers can save a great deal of time if they first identify Power Standards (see Larry Ainsworth's *Power Standards*), and then focus their assessment efforts on the most important standards.

I am currently a principal at a suburban middle school, and we are in the process of developing and implementing common formative assessments. Our leadership team has completed a study of the 2006 book on the subject by Larry Ainsworth and Donald Viegut, and we had a small team attend The Leadership

and Learning Center's common assessment training. As a next step, we are considering collaborative scoring of these assessments. Do you have any general advice for us?

 Here are two ideas to motivate and engage teachers who are working on collaborative scoring. First, calculate the initial level of consensus between the grades teachers are giving. If you have ten teachers scoring a piece of work and six of them say it's a "3," then your consensus level is 60 percent. In general, the more clear the scoring rubric, the higher the level of consensus. Remember, if there is disagreement—and there always is—teachers should not view each other as "the enemy." The only enemy is ambiguity. When teachers work together to reduce ambiguity and improve clarity, the scoring becomes more fair.

Second, calculate time—it's the number one issue that teachers have today. You will be able to build morale and confidence if you can say (with data to back you up), "The first time we tried this, it took us 45 minutes; the second time took 30 minutes; but now we're doing it in less than 15 minutes!"

 I am working with our district to create math quarterly assessments. There has been much discussion about whether we should test all of the power indicators every quarter (using a cumulative model—one question for every power indicator) even though they may not have been taught yet, or whether we should identify the power indicators, create pacing charts, and build quarterly assessments from our pacing charts (using a chunk and build model—with two to three questions per power indicator) for only those power indicators that were taught that quarter. Do you have any documented research to support either one of these designs?

 You'll want to look at Larry Ainsworth's wonderful book *Power Standards* and his more recent work with Donald Viegut, *Common Formative Assessments*.

I'd like to offer three specific points of advice.

First, keep the common assessments *very* short—fifteen to twenty items, with perhaps two extended response items included in that total. That focuses on the most important areas of student learning.

Second, teachers can't assume perfect connection between what they taught and what students know. I've reviewed data sets in which students performed better on items that had not yet been taught than on items that supposedly had been covered. In a twenty-item test, I might include ten items on things I've recently covered, but the other ten might include six to eight items that I thought I covered three to four months ago, and I just want to be sure that students know. The other two to four items might be about new material—information that has not yet been taught, but that some students might know. Remember, the purpose is not to give a grade, but to give both student and teacher good feedback.

If you do want to give the students grades on the test, then you can announce that "the test counts," but only count for grading purposes the seventeen out of twenty items that you actually covered in class.

At the end of the day, feedback is only effective if it is accurate, timely, and specific, so be sure to keep quarterly assessments short enough that students and teachers get the feedback immediately, and ensure that teachers actually use this feedback to make relevant changes in schedule, teaching strategies, and curriculum.

Q 51

In a district-wide standards-based assessment, should directions and questions be read aloud to the students? Or should students read them on their own?

A

The issue of whether or not to read test questions aloud to students is typically a matter of state requirements. It's not a question of whether the assessments are standards-based or not, but rather of giving students the opportunity to experience common testing environments *before* they take the state exam.

For both regular and special education students, the environment of assessment throughout the year should be consistent with what the state requires at the end of the year. Therefore, if students will have instructions read aloud to them in May, then they should receive oral instructional throughout the year. If students must work independently in May and read their own instructions, then that is what should happen throughout the year. Similarly, if students are going to have a "reader" or a "scribe" or any other adaptation or accommodation during the state exam, those should be practiced throughout the year, and not merely used at the end of the year during state testing.

 We are designing pre- and post-testing to measure reading, math, and writing growth over four-week periods. Is it best to use the same exam for both pre- and post-tests? Or should we change the post-test exam so that students don't remember the pre-test items?

Should the same writing prompt be used for both pre- and post-testing? Some teachers are concerned that students will lose motivation to write if the post-test prompt was already used as a pre-test prompt.

 Pre- and post-tests should contain items that are parallel—that is, similar in format and difficulty, but not identical. In math, that is pretty straightforward—keep the item format nearly identical, but change the numbers. Writing is trickier, because, as your colleague notes, students' performance is based on a combination of their writing ability and their knowledge of the prompt. One way to maximize the impact of writing (and minimize the impact of student knowledge of the prompt content) is to increase the number of prompts—perhaps giving students a choice of three prompts for both the pre- and post- test. When students have choice, they have better engagement. Moreover, when teachers are looking at essays with different prompts and content, they are more likely to focus exclusively on the matter at hand—writing—not on the student's knowledge of content from the prompt. There are a number of resources on improved classroom assessment, and I would particularly recommend the work of Tom Guskey, Jane Bailey, Robert Marzano (see especially his new book *Classroom Assessment and Grading That Work*), and Rick Stiggins. One of my books, *Making Standards Work* (3rd ed.) might be useful to you as well, particularly on the issue of creating assessments that are engaging for students. And my book on assessment, *Ahead of the Curve* (2007), includes chapters by Marzano, Stiggins, Guskey, and several other leaders in the field.

I do want to caution that when we try to make classroom assessments too perfect, we make some unfortunate trade-offs. For example, you get higher statistical reliability with more items, but I've seen students and teachers get crushed by eighty-item two-hour tests because a professor told them they need to be "reliable and valid." But a psychometrically perfect assessment that alienates kids and teachers and is so long that the results are not delivered to the students in a timely way is simply a waste of time. Better to do mini-assessments—twelve or fifteen items—that may not have the statistical perfection of eighty items, but where students get same-day or next-day feedback, and teachers use the data in real time to improve instruction. You might get more "perfect" assessments by purchasing them from test companies, but then you're simply paying for the professional development of the employees of test companies instead of using those resources to help teachers design and evaluate good assessments. When teachers create the assessments collaboratively and score them together in a fair and consistent manner, they not only have accurate and timely feedback for students, but they also are much more likely to be aligned with instruction, curriculum, and standards. Teachers will also be emotionally and professionally engaged in assessment, rather than having assessment piled on to the top of an already overflowing plate.

Our district is in the midst of deciding how to weight and record the common assessments that happen twice per year. Our high school educators are happy with the assessments showing on the report card, and with each test counting as five percent of the final grade. The push is to do the same at the middle school level. I am not in favor of this. I want the tests to count as just two percent of the final grade for sixth- and seventh-graders, and I only want it to be shown on the report card for eighth-graders. Our younger students are struggling with the assessments, anxiety-wise and performance-wise. Report cards are very personal to the students, and those students who work very hard, get "B's" for grades and then see a "D" or "F" on a common assessment will be devastated. We have seen this in the classroom when we hand the assessments back to discuss them.

What are your thoughts on the weighting and reporting of common assessments?

First, I reject the premise that the formula for grading must be based on the use of the average. We make fifth-graders learn that the arithmetic mean is not always the best representation of a data set; surely teachers and school leaders can learn the same lesson.

Second, I applaud the notion of making formative assessments "count," but neither these assessments nor *any* single project, paper, assessment, or test should be allowed to profoundly influence a student's grade. Each time teachers assign a "killer project," they administer the academic death penalty. By allowing a single project or test to determine a large portion of students' grades, we are telling students that resilience doesn't matter, that finishing strong doesn't count, and that a single bad week or month can ruin an entire year. Rather than teaching resilience, we teach defeatism.

Therefore, let me offer some practical solutions to this dilemma.

I concur with making the assessments "count"—but only as part of a menu of student projects, assignments, and assessments. If students do poorly on the assessment, the consequence is not failure; the consequence is that students select something else from the menu. The same is true if they miss an assignment, fail a test, or don't complete a project (or, perhaps just as commonly, complete the project, but leave it at the bottom of a locker that resembles a toxic waste dump). The teacher's response should be neither sympathy nor judgment, but simply the rational, logical, encouraging, and firm response that students are responsible for their work, and when they miss important work, they don't fail, but rather they select something else from the menu and *get the work done.* This results in more work of higher quality, better grades, fewer failures, and appropriate respect for formative assessments without making formative assessments "make-or-break" tests.

We are discussing exemption from final exams as an incentive for students to perform well on standardized state testing. Many teachers believe it is not a valid incentive, because those final exams are so important to the kids academically. Others believe the final exam does not have a great value to the student and

that being exempt from it serves as a good incentive to score better on state tests. Do you have any research data on the issue?

I'm aware of no evidence to support the contention that final exams are important to students academically. Lots of tradition and emotion, but no evidence. In fact, there is overwhelming evidence that students—particularly those headed toward college—would be better advised to spend more time on complex nonfiction writing assignments, with lots of feedback and editing. A recent Vanderbilt and Columbia report (Graham & Perin, 2007) reveals that more than half of college students arrive unprepared to meet the demands of college writing. Those are skills that are not met with one-shot final exams.

In fact, there are students who pass the final exam and fail the course, because they failed to do homework; there are students who demonstrate proficiency all year, but choke on the final. The best that can be said of any final exam is that it is one piece of evidence about student proficiency, and not a particularly good piece at that. It's an enormous amount of work for teachers and students, and it is almost *never* used as formative feedback to improve student performance.

The essential question is, "What is the purpose of assessment?" My response is, "To improve teaching and learning." If the test only provides more ammunition for an accounting drill to provide a grade at the end of a semester, then that's a lot of work for not much benefit.

I'm struggling with how to mesh my understanding of learning with the push for standardized testing. At a school this morning, I spoke with a teacher who just reviewed our state's test item selection for science. Our science materials at the elementary level are all hands-on kits, such as Full Option Science System (FOSS), etc. The teacher is asking for a textbook to support her students' learning, because she is sure after seeing the test items that there is no way they can learn what they need to via the kits.

Down the hall, I spoke with another teacher who is piloting Investigations, a research-based math program that supports learning concepts first, then moving to automaticity of

computations. This teacher again was sure that the approach of the Investigations materials would not provide what students need to be successful on our state test.

And I spoke with a principal yesterday who was pushing to purchase more phonic and phonemic awareness drill materials for his students. He wants all students in grades K–3 to be using this phonetic-based process. Again, his reasoning was that we want our students to be successful on our state reading assessment, which tests only individual skills and reading rate.

I know your approach is to turn these conversations into a hypothesis, and ask if we can test them out. For example, "If we teach only computation/textbook-driven materials/drills our students will be successful, whereas if we use hands-on investigations/conceptual learning/problem-solving strategies, our students will not be successful." I have to tell you, it sounds great sitting here at my desk, but very risky when speaking to others.

How can I support the learning and cultural processes that will ensure that all students in our district have a rich learning environment, and also be confident that the students' learning will show positively on state tests?

 Without knowing the details of the specific tests and subjects that you addressed, let me offer some general ideas that I hope can provide the foundation for additional discussion.

First, I think that the teachers have a point. If we are to be held accountable for content, why can't we have texts and curricula to support that content? The less obvious issue, however, is that merely "covering the content" or "having the text" is not necessarily linked to better achievement. For example, my research, along with that of the National Science Foundation and others, suggests that the key to improving science scores is not just more science content, but more literacy and nonfiction writing. Therefore, the impulse to align instruction with assessment is a good one, but the most effective alignment" is not always obvious and direct. The same is true of the reading issue you raised. I think we all agree that phonemic awareness is important, but it is not sufficient. Too many kids are flunking comprehension assessments because they were taught only phonics, not comprehension. Similarly, too many kids never get to comprehension because they lack the fluency that phonics can provide. It's not "either/or"—both are required. Too often, "either/or" thinking sets educators up for failure—either phonics or literature; either computation or problem solving. Every teacher and parent knows that we must do both. Great pianists practice both scales and drills *and* interpretation and art. Great athletes do wind sprints and exercises *and* learn strategy and problem-solving. We can do the same in the classroom.

Second, we can acknowledge the usefulness of tests without submitting to the domination of tests. I try to express this— particularly among skeptical parents and policy makers—by saying something like, "Well, Mr. President, Governor, Superintendent, we'll see you one and raise you ten. We'll show you our test scores, but we'll also show you the other 90 percent of the things going on in our school system." That opens the door to talk about all the non-tested areas—pre-kindergarten, kindergarten, music, technology, art, advanced placement, etc. This means that districts must, without waiting for the state or federal government, develop accountability systems that tell their communities and boards all that they are doing, not just what is reflected on test scores.

Our district is asking that middle and high school teachers give at least one common formative assessment at the end of each nine-week grading period (not the ideal, but a starting point). Principals and teachers feel that this assessment must be part of the students' grades. I have recommended that these assessments count as no more than ten percent of the nine-week grade. Some of our principals feel that it should count as twenty percent of the grade. My feeling is that counting it as no more than ten percent of the grade makes the assessment less punitive—we are supposed to use the results for intervention purposes.

I realize that discussions about grading are always going to be difficult. We have a lot of work to do in this area. Could you please share any thoughts or experiences you have had regarding this subject? I have been charged with gathering information so that we can develop a grading procedure for these nine-week assessments.

The question of percentages is premature. The fundamental question is, "What is the purpose of the common formative assessment?" The answer, I hope, is the same as the answer to any question about assessment, and that is, "The purpose of the assessment is to provide accurate feedback in order to improve performance for students and teachers." Note that the purpose is not to rate, rank, or sort; not to fill a space in the grade book; not to punish slackers or reward the diligent. It is to provide accurate feedback to improve performance.

Once that is clear, then you can make the assessment part of a menu (it counts for students who do well, but those who don't do well have do to more work and select something else from the menu), or make it count in a way that meets administrative requirements but does not create the "academic death penalty" for students who miss it or do badly on it. Before we argue about percentages, let's address the question, "If it doesn't count, then students won't work on it." That's a bone-deep belief, and I respect that, just as I hope that you will respect my earnest belief in the Tooth Fairy. But in both cases, belief does not equal reality, and there is no evidence to support it. Thomas Guskey offers the definitive evidence on this—students, contrary to popular myth, do not perform better when it "counts." Rather, the keys to feedback that leads to better performance are that it be timely, accurate and specific. You'll hear the same refrain from Robert Marzano, Ken O'Connor, myself, and many others.

Video game results are not, to the best of my knowledge, part of a transcript in any middle school, but I know of few middle school students who do not devote more time to video games than to schoolwork. Why? They get feedback that is timely, accurate, and specific. The sole purpose of the feedback is to encourage them to improve their performance—to "get to the next level." The same characteristics of feedback happen in a great music, writing, or math class. It really is about the feedback.

The real answer to "Should the assessment count for ten percent or twenty percent of the grade?" is "That's the wrong question." Both numbers are wrong if students are not getting feedback that improves performance. Both numbers could be right if they are part of a feedback process that encourages students to take the feedback seriously, improve their performance, and therefore improve their scores.

57

I am the principal at a small rural school. We have a population of 259 students from junior kindergarten to grade 8. The number of students in each grade ranges from sixteen to forty. Recently, we received our school results from the government assessment. Based on this data, and other sources of data, we are in the process of developing our school improvement plan. My specific question has to do with sustained growth and how it can be measured at the school level.

One practice that is being suggested is that schools consider last year's assessment data and then set goals relating to those results. As an example, if the grade 3 students last year scored 58 percent proficient in reading, our target this year should be around 65 percent. My concern is that each set of students can be very different, and ignoring those differences makes the practice of setting goals ineffective. I can appreciate that in a large sample size, the differences usually balance out. But in our small school, those differences have a significant impact.

I have been advocating doing comparison of the same students in grade 3 and grade 6, as well as comparing our results to those of other schools. Is there value in comparing grade 3 to grade 6 and our school to the other schools in our region?

Is it reasonable to use a sample size of only a couple dozen students to determine the following year's targets?

You are correct—a "same-student-to-same-student" comparison is the only thing that makes sense. When you have a small sample, comparing this year's fourth grade students to last year's fourth grade students is, well, a comparison of *different* students. It just doesn't work.

 58

I am the principal of elementary special programs, which is an umbrella grouping of many diverse elementary programs such as gifted education, early childhood special education, English Language Learners, and others. We are struggling with finding new ways to collect data that will make a difference. We have been able to find useful data to track early childhood special education—direct instruction to children ages three to five.

My real struggle is gifted education. We have successfully been tracking some data—but in reflecting on that data last week, it's mostly data used to justify our program. Could you suggest data that could be used to track student success? Our gifted program is a full-day pull-out program called Galactic that each grade comes to from all over the district on a different day each week. I feel we cannot take credit for the Measures of Academic Progress (MAP) scores of our students, but I will say that 85 percent of them are proficient or advanced. As well, this last year I took a few of our students who were scoring "Basic" on their MAP mathematics test and signed them up for a math class here at our gifted program to give them a "double dose" of math. I don't yet know the results of that strategy.

We assign no grades to our students, but we do have a lot of accountability, and a "star" system that lets us know if students meet or exceed expectations in each course they take at Galactic.

 I agree that MAP scores are not a great reflection of the success of your students. However, I would not exclude MAP from the equation. One common problem in gifted education is that teachers assume "they already know that," and they fail to give students the grade-level instruction that they need in addition to enrichment opportunities. That's one reason that gifted kids drop out in high school—they have never experienced failure, and then all of a sudden a high school teacher expects them to have some basic skills that they were never taught, because teachers in earlier grades assumed that they had map reading, number operations, and essay construction down pat.

The real question is, as you suggest, what additional measures beyond MAP scores can be used to assess learning?

First, I think you need to stick with "same-student-to-same-student" comparisons, not this year's group to last year's group. That implies, therefore, some sort of pre-instruction and post-instruction test information during the same academic year.

Second, you'll need a variety of instruments, to measure learning, including traditional ones. As David Perkins (1995) reminds us, students who are gifted in one area may not be gifted in others, and therefore the student with superior mathematical ability may nevertheless need traditional literacy tests, or vice versa.

Third, you'll need tests that are sensitive to exceptionally fast progress. That's why tests of a single grade level do not work with gifted students, because even if you give a fifth-grade test to a fourth-grade student, you still have a "ceiling effect" of one year of progress above grade level. More nuanced tests, such as those that use Item Response Theory to give progressively more challenging questions each time a student answers correctly, are better suited for this task. But at the end of the day, you and your colleagues (and students) will complain of test fatigue if you just test the kids all the time.

Fourth, to address the test fatigue issue and also challenge students appropriately, I would favor having them create their own assessments. First, I'd have an honest talk about times when they felt that a test did not allow them to show all that they knew. When a fifth-grader can do algebra, scoring 100 percent on a multiplication and fractions test is not very satisfying. So let them think about different types of assessment—closed-end, open-end, performance, etc.—and have them construct an assessment each month that, if they were the teacher, would allow their students to demonstrate all that they have learned. The worst case is that some kids will sandbag, using this as an opportunity to get out of work by dumbing down the task. I think that risk is minimal, particularly when other students are going to create some wonderfully creative and challenging tasks in a variety of different assessment formats.

CHAPTER 5

Grading, Reports Cards, and Homework

Grading, Report Cards, and Homework

Several schools in my area are asking teachers to make every effort to get a student to make up work before giving a zero. However, they still may eventually give a zero. Does this match with your philosophy? Or should a zero never be given? Also, some of the schools ask teachers to follow this policy, but do not have a mandatory make-up time for students. Teachers just give them extra time to make up the work. What do you think about this?

A This is a critically important issue—one of the most hotly debated in education, and I appreciate the fact that you are willing to explore it. Most people get it wrong, making this a controversy about "zeroes" or "no zeroes," and that completely misses the point. The question is this: What are the most effective consequences that lead to improved student performance? Nobody—least of all me—suggests that there should not be any consequences for missing work or poor performance. The only question is which consequences work most effectively.

If low grades and zeroes were really the most effective consequence, then you'd see every football coach holding a grade book on the sidelines and, when a player made an error, the coach would note it in the grade book, and then mail a negative report to the student six or nine weeks later. But on things that are really important, like football, we don't provide feedback in such a late and meaningless way. Football coaches are famous for providing feedback that is immediate, specific, and designed for only one purpose—an immediate improvement in performance. Teachers can do the same in classes on writing, science, and math, if only they are willing to work as hard as football coaches (and music teachers, who do the same thing with their immediate feedback) do on a daily basis.

To answer your question directly, I would "never say never" about the zero—some students simply will not do the work. But the experience of schools around the nation suggests that we can have a much higher level of student performance (and hence, a much lower number of zeroes) if we have appropriate consequences for missing work. The best consequence, of course, is the requirement that students do the work. Some schools have same-day after-school suspension for any missing assignment. They have a late bus for the football team, and they can also have a late bus for these students. It turns out that alternative transportation is rarely necessary, however, because once students understand that there is a meaningful consequence for missing work (the meaningful consequence is an intrusion on their time, not receiving a zero), then they get the work done. That is why schools that adopt this policy have lower drop-out rates and higher levels of student success. I've documented this extensively in articles and books, in particular in my article "Preventing 1,000 Failures" in the journal *Educational Leadership.*

If teachers must award a zero, then it should be a mathematically accurate zero. On a four-point scale, in which "A" = 4, "B" = 3, "C" = 2, and "D" = 1, the grade for the student who fails to do the work is zero. That is mathematically accurate, because it is an equal interval between each grade. Take a moment and ask yourself—is there any other grade, other than a zero, you would award to a student on this scale? I've never heard a "worse" grade than zero suggested.

But if, as the result of tradition and historical practice, we use a 100-point scale, in which "A" = 90, "B" = 80, "C" = 70, and "D" = 60, what grade is awarded to the student who fails to turn in work? If you answered "zero," then you are claiming that the failure to turn in work is six times worse than doing work wretchedly and receiving a "D," because the zero to 60 interval is six times greater than the "D" to "C" interval of ten points. That is not a logical position. Moreover, returning to the question about the appropriate grade for missing work on a four-point scale, I have never—not once from the literally thousands of teachers involved in these discussions—heard someone suggest, "Well, if they fail to turn in the work, I would award a grade of 'minus six.'" It's absurd on the face of it—but that is logically what they should say if they believe in using zero as a grade on the 100-point scale.

Finally, you got to the heart of the issue when you said that teachers need time to work with students. But don't you find it interesting that teachers and school administrators *always* find the time for teachers to assist and intervene *after* a student has failed, because then the student has to repeat the entire course. Isn't it much more efficient to prevent the failure in the first place?

There will always be those who suggest that we must teach personal responsibility and compliance with the rules, and as a parent and teacher, I agree completely. The only issue is how to most effectively teach these qualities. If, therefore, a regimen of zeroes for missing work is leading to record-high levels of homework completion and student success, and record-low levels of student failures, then by all means, continue that practice. But it is not logical to say "Kids these days just aren't doing homework, they are disorganized, they are late, they are failing … and by the way, I'd like to continue using the same strategies and policies as I've been using for the past twenty years."

In sum, getting rid of the zero is a tiny part of the issue. The central point is providing appropriate consequences to improve student work. My research is unequivocal that when we have appropriate consequences, failures decrease, discipline improves, and more students take and pass not only regular classes, but advanced classes as well. The arguments in favor of the zero as it is commonly used are supported by lots of angry emotion, but I hope that this is a debate that will be resolved by evidence rather than emotion.

I just read your 2004 _Kappan_ article on "The Case Against the Zero," and I believe that you are overlooking an important point, although I understand your argument against disproportionate punishment.

A student assignment is a product, and the letter grade assigned to that product indicates the level of proficiency of the execution of that product. Our grading scale makes the assumption that a certain minimal degree of proficiency will be attained when the assignment is completed.

Personally, I have no problem assigning a zero to a product that never appears, because I received nothing that I asked for. I also don't have a problem bartering with a student if they decide to turn in the assignment later, to make the point that their initial disinterest was ill-advised. I feel that offering half credit on an assignment that is, say, eighteen weeks late in arriving is a generous deal.

Any research that implies that the real world is going to pay me for half the day when I didn't show up to do my work is foolishness. The real world will pay me a full day's wage for a full day's effort, and will dock me pay for any time that I missed.

Training students to live and work in Oz is not what I'm paid to do. In the real world, real lives, real futures, and real undeveloped souls are at stake.

 Here are a couple of ideas for your consideration. First, one of the most important purposes of grading is to provide feedback for improved performance. Perhaps your experience is that the use of the zero has led to students being more diligent and motivated, and if that is the case, you should be experiencing a very high rate of homework compliance and student achievement. That is not my usual observation in schools around the country, but it's very possible that your experience is different than mine.

The second issue is the mathematical one. If your school uses a 4-point grading scale, where students get 4 points for an "A," 3 points for a "B," etc., then awarding a zero for work might be appropriate. But a zero has a dramatically different impact on students' final grades if your school uses a 100-point grading scale. It does not seem to me to be logically consistent to award a zero for missing work on both 4-point and 100-point systems—the difference is not student performance, but only the whim of the district's grading scale.

 I am the principal of a large suburban high school. Our district is working to become standards-based in philosophy as well as in practices. We have made great strides in our elementary schools, but the move to standards-based assessment and grading at the high school level is a bit more challenging.

As a staff we have had the discussion about eliminating the zero in grading. We've read articles and had workshops about this. But the discussion always comes back to: "If there is no zero, what strategies do I have as a teacher to motivate students to do the work I assign?"

If you want to motivate students to do the assigned work, consider a couple of questions:

1. Which teachers in the system already have a high level of compliance with assigned work, and what are they doing that could be useful to others?

2. If the use of zero is not effective in motivating students to do assigned work, then doesn't it make sense to at least attempt some alternative strategies?

Here are two ideas that have worked successfully in other systems and are at least worth a try:

Early final: Administer a "Form B" of the final exam two weeks earlier than the regularly scheduled final. If students have all work complete and earn an "A" or "B" on the early final, then their semester is over. They can't leave campus, but they have earned ten class periods of freedom—something that most teens value very highly. In a school system where that was done in high school science, achievement more than doubled in the first two years this policy was used.

Assignment menu: If students miss an assignment, they don't make it up, or get half-credit, or inundate the teacher with late work—they just choose something else from the menu. 900 points earns an "A"; 800 points earns a "B." If you blow a 100-point test, you can either choose another 100-point item from the menu, or do four 25-point items (it's the teacher's job to ensure that the four 25-point assignments involve at least as much work as a single 100-point assignment. The greatest "danger" here is that students will accumulate enough points for an "A" or "B" before the end of the semester—that's a risk I'm happy to take. In general, rewards for work that is early or on time are more effective than punishments for work that is late.

I'm sure that your teachers have other ideas that might be equally effective.

 I would like to know your thoughts about the following long-standing arguments for retaining the "zero" grade:

1. A grade certifies the percentage of material learned by the student.

2. If a student entirely skips one section out of ten (for example, in a course covering ten different periods of history) and receives a zero grade, this means that the student has learned zero percent of the course material in that section, based on available evidence.

3. Certifying that the student in the above example learned fifty percent of that missed material is inaccurate and unwarranted. Mitigating the zero grade is pragmatically desirable, but giving fifty percent credit based on no evidence is too problematic.

4. A "D" grade almost universally means "present but ignorant." We may not be able to dispense with the "D" in the real world, because of a mixture of social promotion, professorial empathy with someone who has showed up for class, and a bit of professorial cowardice as well.

5. Weighting exams and papers heavier as the term progresses is a good strategy that allows teachers to take into account students' increasing proficiency.

A I'll address these arguments by number:

1. I'm not sure that's accurate. A percentage of 80 in a welding class might leave a student with two missing fingers and a "B"; a percentage of 10 in an art class might leave a student with a masterpiece after nine unsuccessful attempts. Percentages and mastery of the material are not at all equivalent.

2. This may be true in your classes, but in mine, I find that sometimes students "skip" a section and nevertheless learn the material; other times they attend diligently and nevertheless fail to learn a thing. Many zeros, particularly when associated with attendance, have less to do with student learning than with compliance with teacher commands. Perhaps if you changed the context from a class to a faculty meeting, you would agree that attendance and proficiency are not necessarily related.

3. There is a deep mathematical flaw in this reasoning. If we reverted to the nineteenth century practice of "4," "3," "2," "1," "0" grading, then the interval between each grade is the same—that is, the differences between "B" and "C," and "D"

and "F", are both equal to one point. In your example, we are assuming that the difference between "D" (at 60 percent) and "F" (at zero percent for not turning in work) is six times greater than the differences between "D," "C," "B," and "A." I would argue *that* is problematic.

4. I agree. The "D" is, in my view, "the coward's F." But in the real world, "D's" can be eliminated. In fact, I work in schools where the "D" has been eliminated—anything less than "C" work results in failure. The common expectation was that this would magnify the number of "F's." On the contrary, when the "D" was not an option, students worked harder and earned higher grades. This is not "grade inflation," as critics assert, but "performance inflation"—students work harder, learn more, and earn higher grades.

5. It's good that your school allows this; too many have become enslaved by computerized grading systems that diminish the judgment and wisdom of the individual professor.

Our school is under fire from all fronts regarding our new grading policy, which makes the interval between each letter grade the same (7 points); makes 61 the lowest failing grade a student can receive; and tries to eliminate the zero.

Admittedly, we did not do a good job of communicating the new policy to any stakeholder group. As a consequence, our school is in the news practically every day. The latest is that the city council has summoned our administrator and our school board to report the reasoning behind our new grading policy. This is the second time our administrator and school board have been summoned to city council in two months. The mayor hates the new grading policy, and two city councilmen are up for re-election and seem to have selected "improving our educational system" as their battle cry. A recent headline in our area newspaper said our school has gone "From A+ to F." As you know, this is a very *hot* topic.

Can you recommend any articles you or others have written that we could share with city council and the newspaper to support the "eliminating the zero" cause?

My articles "The Case Against the Zero" (*Kappan*, 2004) and, more importantly, "Effective Grading Practices" (*Educational Leadership*, 2008), should be helpful.

Here are the key points in the debate. First, we *all* want students to develop a sense of personal responsibility and a good work ethic—the only question is how to best accomplish that. Second, using the zero on a 100-point scale is a math error, not a political issue. If you discovered a math error in your financial statements, you would fix it, not debate whether or not two plus two equals four. Third, the purpose of grading is to provide feedback for improved achievement. The purpose is not just a grade.

Consider each of these matters in more detail:

Student personal responsibility and work ethic: The critics of your school's new grading policy want to encourage students' personal responsibility and work ethic. *We all agree on that.* The only question is the best way to accomplish this. The zero does not, contrary to the assertions of its proponents, encourage work ethic. In fact, it has the opposite impact. Once a zero is awarded, students learn, "Now I don't have to do the work." If the zero really worked effectively, then the teachers who used it would be seeing record-low levels of failure and record-high levels of homework compliance. I know of very few teachers who are making that claim based on evidence.

It's math, not politics: Not that long ago, grades of "A," "B," "C," "D," and "F" were represented by "4," "3," "2," "1" and "0." That was a mathematically accurate grading policy, with equal intervals between each grade. If the critics of your policy are primarily focused on making sure that students do not receive points for no work, then they should have no problem with going to the 4-point grading system. However, most computer systems default to a 100-point scale rather than 4-point scale, and the 100-point system is the grading system most parents, mayors, and newspaper reporters are accustomed to.

This issue is not about policy or research or politics—it is about mathematical accuracy. It is not mathematically accurate to use a system in which an "F" is six or seven times worse than a "D," and that is what happens when you use the zero on a 100-point scale. This idea is not a new educational fad—it is a return to the work ethic and mathematical intelligence of the nineteenth century. When you fail, the consequences should be respect for teacher feedback, hard work, and the opportunity to try again. Students who fail should not suffer an academic death sentence.

Grading is for feedback, not just evaluation: The purpose of grading is to provide feedback, and the purpose of feedback is to improve performance. When a student fails a driver's examination, he or she retakes the exam. When a student fails to catch a ball, he or she receives feedback from the coach and gets to try again. A football player's touchdowns are not "averaged" in with the "zeros" that resulted from failed catches. On things we care about—like driving and football—we don't use previous poor performances to punish future scores; rather, we give feedback designed to improve performance, we expect the student to respect that feedback and work harder, and then after they achieve the intended result, we celebrate and move on.

If this new type of grading policy were merely "grade inflation," then schools that reform grading policies should have higher grades and lower achievement, as measured externally. But that is not what is happening around the nation. Those schools have higher grades not because of "grade inflation" but because of "performance inflation." Kids are working harder, because the penalty for missing work is not receiving a zero, but having to get the work done. The research on this, which has been principally documented by Dr. Thomas Guskey, goes back to 1911. It's not a new-fangled idea; it is a century old. This is not the twenty-first century "going easy" on kids—it's a return to a good old-fashioned work ethic.

Finally, the sad truth is that there are a lot of people who don't like the idea of more students succeeding. That's one reason that putting more economically disadvantaged and minority kids in advanced placement classes and programs, putting more of "those kids" on honor rolls, and, for that matter, making more of "those kids" capable of going to college and competing for jobs, has never been particularly popular. Effective practices that lead to better results in urban education are not always popular. Changing the penalty for missing work from receiving a zero to having to get the work done is not popular. Students do not thank us for rigor and high expectations, and many other stakeholders do not, either. Our call is not popularity, but effectiveness.

We implemented a "no zero" policy two years ago, and we assign any student who misses an assignment to an after-school study program until the work is completed. Even though this program was designed by a group of teachers, another group of teachers has long resisted it. That group is again complaining and calling the union. I remember hearing you speak about the zero effect at a conference. Is there an article you could point me to that addresses this issue specifically? I would like to get some good research into the hands of some of our faculty members.

See my 2008 article "Effective Grading Practices" in *Educational Leadership*.

I think the essential question is this: How does it help teachers to have more students fail? The people opposing you on this appear to think that having more failures and more students repeating grades is a good idea.

We are developing a ninth-grade intervention pyramid for homework completion. Students would be given no grade penalty if their work is completed within the next day after it is due; if they still do not complete the homework, they may have the opportunity to make up the work after school for half credit. If work is still not completed, parents are contacted and mandatory make-up time is required. Is this a reasonable timeline, or are we moving to half credit too soon?

First, for evidence that your ideas are terrific, just read the September 2007 issue of *Educational Leadership*, published by ASCD (formerly the Association for Supervision and Curriculum Development). More time, great teaching, and multiple opportunities for success—these are the keys to improved achievement. Please also check out my article "Preventing 1,000 Failures" in the November 2006 issue of *Educational Leadership*, and you'll see additional evidence that your ideas are right.

The bottom line is that punishing kids for missing homework doesn't work. The appropriate punishment for missing work is *doing the work*.

There is a broader issue for your consideration, and that is whether "half credit" really is going to be effective and whether that is consistent with the research. For example, if students are graded on a 100 point scale, and a student achieves a 90 on an assignment, but turns it in late, then half credit, or a miserable 45 points, does not encourage the student to do the work. Such a low (and mathematically preposterous) score simply encourages students to give up and conclude that it does not matter how hard they work—they face certain failure. Rather than half credit, consider proceeding immediately with your idea that all students must complete the work before, during, or after school.

 My school is interested in getting rid of the "F." There were a few questions we had for clarification. We have decided to implement six assessments to assist us in determining student achievement, but we have a few questions:
- **What happens to the work that students complete on a daily basis?**
- **How is that daily work assessed?**
- ***Should* students' daily work be assessed?**

 Eliminating the "F" is a wonderful goal, though I'd happily settle for a dramatic reduction in the number of "F's," recognizing that some students may call your bluff.

With regard to your specific questions—daily work *should* be assessed. For guidelines on the effective use of homework, see Robert Marzano's *Classroom Instruction That Works.* I also have had great success with homework menus, offering students choices of assignments.

When students fail to complete daily work (or they lose it, or the dog ate it, etc.) then the appropriate consequence is not an "F," but rather the requirement that students *do the work.* Some schools have "quiet tables" at lunchtime. Others restrict privileges in study hall, home room, and academic advisory periods—any students who don't complete their work lose the privilege of choosing activities during those periods. They must do their homework instead. Others create time before, during, and after school for work. Others have immediate same-day after-school suspension for students to get their homework done. As one of my principals told me, "The word 'homework' may or may not have anything to do with the word 'home'—because some kids go home to private rooms, stereos, and moms who help with homework, and other kids go home to chaos."

You have said that students should always be given credit for the assignments that they do, even if they are late. You also said that students should always be made to do the work regardless of when the assignment was due. What are your thoughts on grading a student who is given multiple opportunities to complete an assignment and still chooses not to? Should that student receive a zero for that assignment? How should the missed assignment be calculated into a marking period grade? Finally, have you found that some students choose not to work as hard because they know that missing work or lower grades are easier to make up on future assessments?

First, we all agree that students should have consequences for late and missing work. The only question is *what* the consequences should be. The most common consequence, of course, is the withholding of credit. If that is working for students—if your teacher comments and grading data suggest that you have record-high levels of compliance with homework—then I'd encourage you to continue this practice. If that's not the case, then a different consequence is called for. A better consequence is to require that students do the work. Some students, as you point out, may be defiant and never do it. I'm not suggesting that my ideas work 100 percent of the time, but if our strategies can get homework compliance from 20 percent to 70 percent, then I wouldn't fail to implement them just because of that last 30 percent. Moreover, you can consider implementing other consequences, such as placing restrictions on free time for missing work, and, more powerfully, granting extra free time for work that is done well and on time.

Second, I'm not suggesting necessarily that students do the *same* assignment as the one they failed to turn in—though that may be appropriate in some cases. Rather, I'm suggesting that students do appropriate work that shows evidence of learning. It's simply not the case that homework is always evidence of learning. Often, it is nothing more than evidence of compliance with teacher demands—that's why one student can earn an "A" or "B" on a final and fail the class due to missing work, and another student can earn a passing grade in the course for "effort"—i.e., complying with teacher requirements—but never be proficient in the course.

Third, if all else fails and you must assign a zero, then at least make it an accurate zero. On a four-point scale, where "A" = "4," "B" = "3," etc., a zero is accurate, because the difference between the "A," "B," "C," "D," and "F" are all equal—one point. But assigning a zero on a 100-point scale is a math error it implies a 60-point difference between the "D" and "F," while the other differences are typically about 10 points. It makes missing a single assignment the "academic death penalty." It's not just unfair—it is not mathematically accurate.

Fourth, the idea that students will delay work because they can turn work in late without consequence is a very reasonable fear, and a hypothesis that is worth testing. The easiest way I know of to test that is to ask whether, in classes that gave zeros for missing work and did not allow submission of late work, if students responded by turning in work on time and proficiently, and therefore those teachers had the highest passing percentages in your school. But that's not usually what I find. Teachers who claim that "students will sandbag us" think that they have adolescent psychology figured out—but their own data do not support their conclusions. The "menu" system, which is explained in the Leadership and Learning Center's *Effective Grading Practices* seminar, gives students incentives to get their work done on time—even early—and to do it proficiently. Students *crave* freedom and choice—those are the motivators we should tune into. The overwhelming consensus of the research, literally since 1911 (see Thomas Guskey's work on this) is that grading as punishment does not work.

I realize that this is a very difficult and contentious subject, particularly among high school faculty. At the end of the day, it's not what I say that matters, but what your own research and your own data suggest. The key is to heed that data. It is irrational for an educator to say, "Students are not turning work in, are late, are disrespectful, and are not passing my class," and at the same time to insist that they should use the same teaching, assessment, feedback, and grading practices that have led to this state of affairs. If the high school football coach continued to use strategies that did not work, he wouldn't be coaching for long.

Our school district eliminated "D" grades in 2002. The premise at the time was that anything less than a 70 percent in a class would result in an "F," and the student would receive no credit for the class.

Now, the district is taking another look at the policy and considering reinstating the "D" grade, because many students fall in the 65–69 percent range, which is close to a "C."

Can you refer me to any studies on this topic? I would like our PTA to take a position, but I want to make sure they are as informed as possible.

I think the most compelling study that you would be able to do about this would be to look at the performance of a group of students who scored a "D" (that is, they passed) before the "D" was eliminated, and then observe what happened to them the *next* year.

One study, which I wrote about in *Educational Leadership* in the 2007 article "Teachers Step Up," focused on eighth grade in particular. The district (which won the Malcolm Baldridge National Quality Award) learned that if a student received either an "F" or a "D" in English, or an "F" or a "D" in math, they had more than a 90 percent probability of failing ninth grade math the next year. When the district moved to effective interventions for those ninth grade students with "lab" classes (twice the time, intensive intervention, highly qualified teachers), in a single year the failure rate for the "lab" students was lower than the failure rate for the "regular" students.

But there are two deeper issues in your question that I think must be addressed. Just addressing the numerical mechanics of grading does not accomplish very much unless you also address the structural issues of instructional decisions behind the grades.

First, there are two possible consequences when a student does nonproficient work. One is a low grade (whether it is a "D" or an "F" doesn't really matter). The other consequence is getting feedback, improving performance, and becoming proficient at the "C" or higher level. Schools that make the former choice see the teacher as "judge, jury, and executioner"—grades are terminal evaluations, and that's it. Schools that make the latter choice see the teacher as the person who gives feedback to improve student performance. Music teachers, football coaches, and technology teachers all operate in the latter manner, giving feedback to improve performance, and not "averaging" the mistakes of September into the final grades of December.

Second, the example presumes a 100-point scale, which is a mathematical distortion. We used to have 4-point scales, in which an "A" was a "4," "B" was a "3," "C" was a "2," "D" was a "1," and if a student missed an assignment, they received a zero. There were equal intervals between all grades. If you use a 100-point scale, a student could have the identical performance and have a signifi-cantly different grade. Why? Because on the 100-point scale, the "D" is typically worth 60 points, but a missed assignment remains a zero, thus creating a dramatically larger (and inaccurate) interval between the "D" and zero in the 100-point system than in the 4-point system. I elaborate on this more in the 2008 *Educational Leadership* article "Effective Grading Practices."

This is one of the most important issues in education now. Schools can do a lot of things right with standards, curriculum, and teaching, but when they use grading practices that are ineffective, it undermines everything else the teachers and administrators are attempting to accomplish.

I am writing about a new dual grading concept that our high school is currently developing. I want to share with you what I believe is a novel grading concept, and to inquire if you perceive any unintended negative outcomes.

For the last two years, our school has been engaged in transitioning into a Professional Learning Community. The first year was devoted to forming professional collaborative teams, identifying power standards, and creating common assessments. This year, our focus was on interventions and formative assessments. Next year, we will be addressing the challenge of grading reform. We took initial steps toward grading reform the second semester of this year, by eliminating zeros, eliminating extra credit, accepting late work, and diminishing unnecessary

"busy work."

We are proposing a dual grading concept. The idea is to report two separate grades for each course: one grade for academic achievement (summative assessments), and a second grade for personal management (homework, class work, and participation). Credit towards graduation will be awarded solely based on the academic grade. Grade Point Average will be calculated with 75 percent from the academic grade and 25 percent from the personal management grade.

The provosts from several state universities have been supportive and encouraging about our new grading concept. Universities have expressed interest in data that will be available for analyzing determinative student characteristics for successful undergraduates.

What do you think of this concept? What should we be thinking about that we are not currently considering? Do you foresee any unintended consequences of this grading method?

 I think that your proposed grading system represents a reasonable compromise, including both student proficiency in the academic area and also considering the work ethic and personal responsibility of students. I particularly endorse the way that you have addressed some of the worst grading practices—using zeros on a 100-point scale, using averages, and assigning meaningless homework.

I have a couple of observations about possible unintended consequences for your consideration.

First, the proposed weighting of each grade in the GPA implies that a student who earns perfect scores on tests of proficiency but failed to turn in homework would have a final grade of 75—a "D" or "F" in many schools. The issue in things that matter—from basketball to music to English—is performance. I think that as teachers we have to use homework for what it is—practice to improve performance. Just as in music and basketball, different students need different types and amounts of practice.

I understand that this policy may represent a political compromise with those who believe that the most important thing that students do is comply with teacher directives, rather than demonstrate proficiency in the subject. So rather than argue that point, I recommend that you and your colleagues gather data. Plot student results in two columns: the first representing homework and the second representing performance. See what the relationship is between the two columns by plotting one on the "X" axis and the other on the "Y" axis. I think you'll see a strong, but not perfect, correlation. Then the question we address as teachers is, "What do we do with the outliers?" That is, what about the students who have great performance, but lousy homework compliance, or great homework, but lousy performance? You'll learn a great deal from these questions and also convey that you are open-minded teacher-researchers.

Second, what creativity and flexibility is there within the system? I think that you have created some thoughtful and appropriate boundaries. Nevertheless, I can envision many different ways that teachers will apply those boundaries. Use that flexibility as a treasure trove of research, and use next semester's data to explore your best practices. Specifically, create some benchmarks, such as this fall's pass rates, GPAs, discipline rates, etc., then compare those benchmarks to the rates achieved by the same teachers in the same classes next fall, looking for "positive deviance," in the words of Kerry Patterson et al, authors of *Influencer* (2008)—a great book that I recommend. I think you'll find that it is not just the policy itself, but also the creative and thoughtful way that teachers apply the policy that makes a difference.

Finally, I'm sure that the Board of Education will pose some thoughtful questions based on a sincere desire to improve the personal responsibility of students. Any change to grading systems engenders such challenges. Therefore, I encourage you to respond in a positive way to these challenges. It is important to convey that this is not just about grading policy, but also about appropriate consequences for student work that is excellent and student conduct that is irresponsible. We know that it's not effective to punish students for great work or to reward students for lousy conduct. Your proposed policy recognizes this. For example, when we flunk proficient students in June because of homework failures in January, we are punishing resilience, learning, and respect for teacher feedback. When we give students credit for work that is lousy but on time, we reward sloppy work. When we give students zeros for missing work, we reward poor conduct. If you don't believe that the zero is a "reward" just ask the kids—they tell me all the time, "gimme the zero." I refuse to do so, and instead require that they actually do the work. The board needs to know that your policy represents not leniency and a "soft" approach, but greater rigor and more effective consequences.

What is your view on students being graded on "participation" in physical education classes?

Certainly participation is a part of any assessment—you need to show up in order to be assessed. But I don't think that it should be the only criterion. While I'm certainly not an expert in the field of physical education, a few additional criteria might include:

1. Setting personal fitness goals, tracking improvement, and demonstrating commitment toward progress
2. Learning new games and activities and demonstrating an understanding of rules and sportsmanship
3. Analyzing game strategy (perhaps in a written response)
4. Teamwork—assisting others in a meaningful way

If the "participation" grade is an attempt to avoid inappropriately grading down students who lack physical skills, I appreciate the motivation, but I disagree with setting low expectations. Students do not need to be star athletes, but they do need to engage actively in the class and learn new skills.

In my class, students must track late assignments with a "Late Assignment Sheet" that is filled in the first day they don't turn in the assignment. After the second day of not turning in the assignment, students must fill out the form and phone their parents. On the third day, I phone their parents, and the form is filled out. I cease to "chase" the kids around after the third day. They do not receive a late mark or any other consequence, although we do talk about how their character is developing. Is this "talking-to" enough? I am finding that a small group of students will turn in their work on day three regardless, and I worry that I am perpetuating irresponsibility by not providing harsher consequences.

Have you found that, on the whole, more students are turning in more work (even if it is a day or two late) than was the case before you had this policy in place? What, in your judgment, is the alternative for the small group of students that you describe who are turning in the work on day three? What portion would simply never hand in the work at all?

I think that your answers to these questions might suggest that the focus of your energies should be on your excellent teaching, motivation, and strategies. You will have some lazy kids who avoid homework and take advantage of your good nature. But I wouldn't sacrifice your otherwise excellent ideas just because a small group is failing to appreciate your lessons in project management and character.

In sum—you're right, and don't let the occasional bad apple get you down. You're using thoughtful guidance, not punishment, and that's a wise strategy.

 What does research say about students missing recess in order to finish their incomplete homework?

 Let's start with Robert Marzano's meta-analysis on the value of homework (2007). As much as kids and many parents hate to hear it, "homework works." It's good for practice and useful for reinforcement of essential skills. Of course, Bob does not endorse just any homework, but rather homework that meets specific criteria, including the development of skills that have already been introduced and the opportunity for students to say "I got stuck here" and seek additional help.

Next, we need to consider the words of my first principal, who said, "Homework may or may not have anything to do with the word 'home.'" This strikes at the heart of your question. If kids come to school without their homework done, is that because they are lazy and disorganized, or because Donna Reed has yet to check into their homes and look inside their backpacks? It's just not right (and is educationally bankrupt) to punish children for the errors of their parents, or reward children for the diligence of their parents. Therefore, I would argue that wise teachers create time during the school day, but outside of recess and lunch, in which there is "choice"—some students "choose" to do homework during that time, and other children "choose" different activities. It's an appropriate incentive. "If I get my work done before school, then I can make a different choice," the reasoning should go.

Finally, what about the inevitable argument, "But you haven't seen *this* kid!" OK—the kid doesn't get homework done at home, won't do it during "choice" time, and is generally a pain. If the kid is a seventh grader, the clinical diagnosis for that condition is called "normal," and we need to get over it. It's my responsibility—and I've done it a thousand times as a teacher—to give the student no choice except to do the work.

Let's also challenge the notion that recess is a bucolic and delightful pastime full of unremitting glee. It's a time of terror, bullying, and fear for a lot of kids, and the choice to stay inside and do homework is entirely rational and reasonable. The "recess is wonderful" crowd needs to give it a rest—some kids do well in unstructured play time and others do not. We know that differentiated attention to the needs of the individual child is a smart idea inside the classroom; the same is true on the playground.

Perhaps the best way to resolve this issue is the simple question, "Is it working?" If the use of contrived free time, differentiated recess, or other strategies is effective, then great—keep it up. If those strategies are not resulting in better student achievement, then be willing to experiment with alternatives.

Our school is in its second year of using a standards-based reporting system. We have factored out nonacademic areas, effort, behavior, etc. We have broken the subject areas into broad standards such as geometry, computation, number sense etc. (specific standards under each of the latter broad categories are not included.) Last year, we decided to use year-end standards as the reference point and rated students in relationship to those standards, (with the exception of science and social studies which were more close-ended units). So at the beginning of the year, more kids had "2's," and as the year progressed, the kids got closer to the standard and many "2's" became "3's" or "4's." This year, many teachers feel they should rate the students based only on the content presented by the end of the assessment period.

So, for example, there would be more "3's" given right now in computation, because the students did well with addition and subtraction (the only computation skills instructed thus far), rather than giving students "2's," reflecting progress towards the year-end standard that includes multiplication, division, decimals, etc. The inconsistency and confusion is a problem, and we are willing to learn and grow. What is your advice?

First, congratulations to you and your colleagues for addressing these incredibly important issues. Too many schools just ignore these complexities and allow each teacher to communicate grades in an entirely different way, leaving students and parents completely confused. The fact that you are willing to engage in this struggle is a mark of professionalism.

Here are my observations about the issue:

1. Rating students based on year-end expectations is the right thing to do. It essentially says to students in the fall, "You are not proficient yet—that's why you come to school." Saying that a student is not proficient does not mean that he or she is a failure or that the teacher is inadequate. It just is stating the truth—that there is work to be done between now and the end of the year.

2. Rating students on progress up to the current point is fine, too. Think of helping a teenager to learn how to drive. I *heaped* praise on my 16-year-old for getting across the parking lot without any damage to people or property. But at the same time, I didn't call her "proficient" or in any way inflate her driving "grade" until she had truly mastered that skill. Similarly, I can tell my students that they can be justifiably proud of their progress, but also challenge them appropriately by pointing out that there is a huge distance between where they are now and where they need to be in the spring.

3. Separate rating from progress. If a rating is to be reliable, it needs to be like a scale in the grocery store—it doesn't change based on the season, or on how sympathetic the grocer is to my needs. A scale is just a scale, and it gives me a consistent and accurate measurement. Don't confuse your rubrics, assessments, and other scales with progress measurements. Make it OK with students, parents, and teachers to say, "*Great*

progress, and not yet proficient"—an honest, consistent, and accurate statement.

I have an issue in my school and need some advice. I am trying to implement sound grading practices—giving students descriptive feedback and chances to retake tests and redo work to show mastery, etc.—based a lot on the work of Ken O'Connor and Rick Stiggins.

But I am getting a *huge* negative reaction from parents of honors students. For example, I received a challenging e-mail that contained the following points:

1. **Student A receives a 92 on the first test, but student B receives a 70. When student B retests, he receives a 95, which beats student A, who did well on the first test. You are penalizing student A for doing what he/she was supposed to do, and rewarding student B for not getting the job done the first time. All that aside, how do you handle the class rank in such a situation? It looks to me like student B ends up with the higher GPA, and you know that's not fair.**

2. **Teacher A decides not to follow this new program, but teacher B is following the program. Students in Teacher B's classes have the opportunity to receive a higher GPA than students in Teacher A's classes, because they have multiple chances to do their work and retake their tests. Again, this seems unfair. If, on the other hand, you are going to assure parents that all chemistry honors classes, regardless of the teacher, are not using the new program, then we are back to a level playing field.**

How do you suggest that I respond to the GPA/Class Rank question? (By the way, students who take honors classes are on a 5 point scale—they receive an extra quality point for being in honors classes. So students can get all "A's" and never make the top 10 if they don't take honors classes.)

I greatly admire the work of Ken O'Connor and Rick Stiggins, and endorse their approach. The Leadership and Learning Center is offering a new seminar called *Effective Grading Practices* that includes their work, along with the work of Robert Marzano, myself, and others.

First, I recommend that you express appreciation to any parent who is willing to become engaged in these issues. Too many parents are either disengaged completely from high school, or limit their communication to complaints. The points above invite a thoughtful dialog. Let the parent who sent them know you appreciate that.

Regarding the first example above, there are several points to consider:

1. Nothing stopped student A, who received a 92, from re-testing and attempting to get a 100. Great teachers challenge everybody, not just those who go from 70 to 95, but those who started with a 92 and, rather than becoming complacent, work harder and do even better.

2. The premise is that one student "did what he was supposed to do" and the other did not. That is one possibility. A far more likely possibility, in my experience, is that students come to class with very different levels of background and preparation. Our job as teachers is to do all that we can to make students proficient by the end of the semester. If this were the track team, nobody would be surprised that the coach decides who goes to the state finals based on how team members are running at the end of the semester—not based on their average throughout the semester. Similarly, in algebra, music, science, and art, our goal must be to challenge students for continually improved performance throughout the year. In driving class, we don't settle on an average, but insist that students master skills before we let them on the road. For some, it takes longer, but we don't have different "grades" of licenses.

3. With regard to GPA and class rank and fairness, the essence of a fair system is that all students have the opportunity to succeed. Some students—the tortoises like me—will perhaps start slow, but finish ahead of their peers who started well, but never challenged themselves. That is quite fair, as long as everyone had the same opportunity to improve. I challenge the premise that the difference between a 3.674 and 3.673 GPA is as great as students and parents think it is. Yes, I know that transcripts are important, But they are not as important

as you might think. Have conversations with college admissions officers to see what I mean.

Colleges regularly reject students with 4.0 grade point averages and perfect SAT scores. This is not urban legend, but a fact confirmed recently by Tufts University admissions counselors during a recent (April 2010) visit in which I accompanied a high school student who was considering applying at this very selective school.

Colleges, including the most competitive ones, are looking not only for transcript grades, but for evidence of students who seek challenges, show leadership, display creativity, and have an ethic of service. A growing number of schools are using the Harvard system, in which there are three categories of honors—highest honors, high honors, and honors. The traditional high school farce of the difference between the valedictorian and the salutatorian being that the latter took 9th grade band and therefore didn't get a quality point must, at some point, be seen for what it is—a distinction without a difference.

4. Perhaps the most important issue is this—the fundamental purpose of assessment and evaluation is *not* rendering a judgment. The fundamental purpose is *improving student performance.* In the example above, the teacher clearly did that, using the grade of 70 as a wake-up call and the opportunity to re-take the exam as a spur to more work and improved performance. That is *exactly* what we expect great teachers, coaches, and leaders to do.

Regarding the second example above, what would you do if you had a new policy for crosswalk safety, but crosswalk guard A decided "not to follow this new program." What about a cafeteria manager who says, "Asking me to change the way I do hygiene is infringing on my personal freedom." Is the analogy of grading policy to student safety and health appropriate? If you don't think so, ask yourself if students who succeed in high school have different safety and health risks, both during their teenage years and in their occupations later in life, than students who do not succeed and eventually drop out. The fundamental attributes of any effective grading policy are fairness (and that means that different teachers give the same grade for the same performance), effectiveness (teachers have evidence that the grading policy leads to improved performance), and accuracy (it can't be accurate when the same performance by the same student could result in different grades).

Whatever system you design—particularly if you are locked into the alchemy of quality points—will lead to a couple of things: students who try to game the system, and college admissions officers who have complete contempt for it. That is the reason that, unfortunately, more and more emphasis is placed on students' scores on standardized tests such as SAT, ACT, AP, and IB. People know that GPAs generally are inaccurate.

 75

In our elementary and middle schools we are developing a standards-based report card. We are also interested in moving in this direction in the high school, but are finding that we are facing a lot of resistance from faculty and parents. It would be very helpful if we had some stories about schools that have successfully implemented standards-based reporting that we could examine and share. Can you make any suggestions?

There are quite a number of success stories of standards-based report cards, but I would caution that parents are most likely to accept this new system when they perceive it as adding value to their communication from teachers rather than subtracting from it. If, for example, parents are used to letter grades, and those marks are replaced by a standards-based achievement report (see an example in my book *Making Standards Work*), then parents (and students) ask, "What was my grade *really*? Was it a 'B' or an 'A' or what?" If, by contrast, parents receive both the grade and a standards achievement report, then they know not only what the grade was, but how the grade was earned. There are a number of excellent resources on this. The Leadership and Learning Center is offering a new seminar called *Effective Grading Practices*. I would also recommend the work of Thomas Guskey and Jane Bailey, Ken O'Connor, and Robert Marzano, all of whom have written thoughtfully about this issue. Their books also contain examples of standards-based reports.

I am the mother of two middle school girls. Our school administration recently introduced a new progress report and potential report card system that would reflect a system called "standards-based reporting." Can you tell me about the effectiveness of this type of program for progress reports and report cards? Parents here are skeptical about giving up letter grades in favor of this type of program. We live in a very small rural community, and our school houses just 547 students in grades K–8. Our state standardized test scores are extremely low compared to the rest of the state. Any feedback would be much appreciated. I have read your book *Crusade in the Classroom* and felt you would be able to provide some advice on this topic.

First, I want to suggest that we need not have an "either/or" controversy here. It's not a choice between *either* letter grades *or* standards-based reporting. If parents want to have letter grades, then teachers can provide them. But the key is that letter grades need to be accurate, specific, related to real student achievement, and designed to improve achievement. Unfortunately, most letter grade systems fail to meet any of those requirements.

Thomas Guskey wrote a great book called *How's My Kid Doing?* That is the fundamental question, and I think we should take Tom's question seriously.

For example, if a child is getting honor roll grades, but cannot pass a basic literacy or math exam, that suggests to me that teachers are awarding grades based on behavior, not achievement. On the other hand, if a child is failing school, but getting wonderful scores on final exams and external tests, that suggests to me that a child is being scored on compliance with homework requirements and teacher demands rather than genuine proficiency.

I think the school system should consider doing both: reporting students' achievement on standards *and* providing a letter grade. Then parents can ask some tough questions, such as, "If my kid is getting an 'A' or 'B,' why is my kid failing an external assessment? Is that just because my kid is pleasant and nice?" or "My kid is failing the class—look at all the 'D's' and 'F's' and comments about bad behavior—but can you help me understand why this is the case when my kid is acing the external tests in math and reading?"

Our district is gearing up to begin using standards-based report cards for the next school year. They would be implemented in grades K–4 in our district.

The third- and fourth-grade report card that has been designed currently has teachers assessing the standards (with a four-tier evaluation system) and *also* giving a letter grade in each subject area. What is your opinion on using "traditional grades" and standards-based assessments on the same report card? The teachers worry that parents will be confused between a student receiving a "B" grade and a "B" for beginning.

I can certainly understand the confusion about using the letter "B" to represent two different levels of proficiency. However, based on what I have seen in arguments over report cards in many districts, I believe that you and your colleagues were *very wise* to preserve, at least for a transition period, the traditional letter grades. What has happened too frequently across the country is that the standards-based report cards, which were implemented with the best of intentions, to give parents accurate and meaningful information about their children, hit a brick wall of resistance, because parents believed that they were "losing" the feedback with which they were most familiar—traditional letter grades. When new report cards are implemented, the most common question is, "What is it *really*? Is it an 'A?'"

I'd like to offer a few ideas to consider. First, ensure that parents are involved in the redesign of the report card. They can not only help avoid confusion, but also help communicate things to other parents. They will also help school leaders avoid the jargon that too frequently creeps into standards-based report cards. The "gold standard" is a report card that students can explain to parents without assistance from the teacher. That implies, for example, that it probably isn't a good idea to use the term "phonological awareness" on a first grade report card.

Second, consider a transition period that includes both the old and the new, at least for a limited period of time. Ultimately, you would hope that parents would eventually say, "Why are you using the old letter grades? We get much better information from this standards-based report card." In Riverside, California, for example, that transition took five years.

Third, don't try to evaluate every standard. You might consider reading Larry Ainsworth's *Power Standards*, so that you can narrow the focus to only a few standards that have the greatest impact on student achievement.

Finally, ask teachers in the next higher grade what skills and knowledge are most important for students entering their classrooms next year. In my experience, they almost always mention at least a few things that are not on the report card. So, for example, if the fifth-grade teachers are saying that one of the five or six most important things for students to know and be able to do before fifth grade is to create and maintain an assignment notebook, then I would put that skill on the report card. If sixth-grade teachers say that nonfiction writing is particularly important, then I would not just have a single grade for "writing," but would distinguish creative writing, at which many elementary students excel, from nonfiction writing, which is infrequently assigned and assessed in many elementary schools.

In the meantime, why not use "N" for "Novice" rather than "B" for "Beginning," and save yourself a lot of communication challenges?

 Q 78

My school is working towards our first reporting period using a standards-based reporting system. In our old grading method, kids who got "A's" and "B's" were listed on the honor roll. Under the new grading system, teachers are getting hung up on trying to give "3's" (on a 4-point scale where "3" means "meets the standard") so the kids can be on the honor roll. I am afraid this will derail the progress we are making, because the pressure to give a 3 so a student can be on the honor roll may lead teachers to give that rating, rather than accurately rating students whose learning is still developing (especially early in the year) by giving them a 2 (which means "learning in progress"). Can you suggest how we can align student recognition with a standards-based system?

The question is, "What if a student—special education or otherwise —is reaching his or her objectives, but still not meeting the standard?" My response is that we should stop punishing teachers (and kids and parents) for being honest. It's entirely possible (and necessary) for a teacher to say, "Doug is not meeting the fourth-grade writing standard yet") and also to say, "Doug met six out of his eight objectives (IEP objectives, learning objectives, or other established objectives), and therefore Doug is eligible for the honor roll."

In other words, teachers should reward work ethic, progress, and meeting short-term objectives with the honor roll—but they should not tell parents children are "meeting a standard" when in fact they are "making progress" and are not yet meeting the standard.

The key is to work with parents so that they know that neither they nor their children are losing anything with regard to recognition and respect for their hard work, and that they also know that teachers are working hard to give the parents accurate and complete information. As I try to say to parents in the fall, "Of *course* he's not proficient yet—that's why he's in school!" I try to do this with a smile and encouragements, and develop a relationship that says, "Any time we tell students they are not proficient, we always add the word 'yet' to the end of the sentence."

We are looking for source information to support the premise that having students rewrite an essay several times to achieve a higher level of quality is a better practice than asking students to write multiple essays that are each graded once and returned to the students.

Here are several research sources about the relationship between student writing, editing, and rewriting, and improved student achievement.

My work on the topic includes:
• *Accountability for Learning*
• *The Daily Disciplines of Leadership*
• *101 Questions and Answers About Standards, Assessment, and Accountability*

In addition, the specific issue of feedback that results in improved student performance—formative feedback—has been addressed in the following:

- *Educative Assessment*, by Grant Wiggins
- *Classroom Instruction That Works*, by Robert Marzano et al.
- *Assessment for Learning*, by Stiggins, Arter, Chappuis & Chappuis.
- *The Art of Teaching Writing*, by Lucy Calkins

I am having difficulty convincing my staff that allowing students to retake tests and giving credit for redone homework is appropriate. They are hung up on the responsibility/citizenship issue, and I also believe they don't like the idea because they don't want more work. I can mandate these practices, but I would like to present my staff with data supporting them.

First, I want to express my complete agreement with your staff. We all agree that responsibility and citizenship are good ideas. Kids *should* have appropriate consequences for failure to do homework or complete projects, and for doing badly on tests. The only questions are how best to encourage responsibility and citizenship, and what the appropriate consequences should be.

This is very important—don't start with the perspective "I'm right and the teachers are wrong." Start with the perspective that you, your staff, and I all love kids, care about them, and want them to grow up with a good sense of responsibility and citizenship. From that common ground, let's ask some questions:

1. Are our present practices leading students to improve their rates of homework completion and classroom success? If so, then let's just check the data: what was the percentage of failures five years ago? Three years ago? Last year? If our strategies are effective, then failures—particularly failures due to the failure to complete homework—should be declining significantly. But that's not, in fact, what I see around the country. Typical grading practices—giving students "zeroes" for missing work, refusing to take late work, refusing to allow students to resubmit work, the use of the average—are not resulting in improved performance. In fact, teachers complain to me all the time that students are not completing work, that they are disengaged and nonresponsive. In other words, if our

goal is improved citizenship and responsibility, what we are doing now apparently is not working very well.

2. What alternatives have we tried? In almost every school, I find wide variation in teacher grading practices. There are some teachers who, quietly and almost anonymously, have been experimenting with different practices. Before you consider anything I have to say, conduct a "treasure hunt" by analyzing the classes where failure rates have declined and achievement has improved. Look in different departments around the district where success is high—often driver's education, music, computer programming. What do those areas have in common that we can learn from? One thing that I know is true in all three is that when you make a mistake, it doesn't lead to failure, but rather to listening to teacher feedback, respecting teacher feedback, improving performance, and ultimately passing the assessment.

3. What will be our criteria for making a decision about grading practices? Can we at least agree that even if people are skeptical about adopting new practices, we'll let the evidence be our guide? I've worked in very remote parts of Africa where people did not believe that vaccinations were effective. They didn't want to see my studies or hear a lecture on western medicine. But they were willing to look at children who lived or avoided horrible lifelong disabilities because they didn't get polio. The evidence, not my beliefs or their beliefs, ultimately allowed for more vaccinations. So in our schools, can we agree that even if we're not sure, we'll at least try some experiments, and then let the evidence decide? I think that teachers are smart, and that they care about kids and love them. But they are skeptical—they don't want to see another "hot idea" come and go. So, let's take our time, but let's try new methods, and have the intellectual integrity to let the evidence, and not personal feelings, determine which are the best practices.

4. Can we agree on some fundamental values? Even if we disagree on policy, can we agree on values such as fairness? Can we agree that grading practices should not be based upon subjective appraisals that can be influenced by gender, race, economic status, or parent activism? Can we agree that

the central purpose of feedback, including grades, is the improvement of student achievement?

5. What's in it for the teachers? Can we agree that if we can implement policies that will reduce our failure rate, that we would have happier, more engaged, and better-behaved students? Can we agree that if we have fewer students repeating grades and courses, we'll have fewer angry and bored students?

6. What's in it for the school and community? Can we agree that if we have fewer students repeating math and English, that ultimately we'll have more opportunities for art, music, technology, service learning, and other things that both students and teachers find engaging and worthwhile?

Once you have settled these questions, try some experiments. Perhaps different teachers could try different things. Some might just eliminate the zero. Some might stop using averages to determine grades. Others might try a "menu" system, where the consequence for missing work or failing a test is selecting other items from the menu to earn points. Others might experiment with giving rewards for work that is on time or early rather than punishment for work that is late.

In other words, I'm not asking you to use *my* system, but rather that you use your good judgment and the thoughtful goodwill of your colleagues to: a) Admit that current practices could be improved; b) Experiment with different ideas that improve achievement and reduce failures; and c) Agree that the final school-wide decision will be based on evidence and not personal prejudices.

My son is in second grade. He wrote a one-page paper about his town and drew a picture. His teacher graded it by circling the incorrect grammar, and at the bottom of the page she subtracted three points for errors, out of a total of seven points. He received three points overall, which left him with a grade of 43 percent, which she wrote on top of the paper in red, with a big fat "F" beside it. I spoke to her about this and she stated that some kids do better when they see an "F." My response was that I did not want to see any grade letter at all on top of his papers, especially if it was an "F," but that the percentage would suffice. She also

has the students write their name 50 to 100 times if they forget to put their name on their papers. Please tell me what you think of this.

 My heart breaks for your son, who appears to be stuck in a situation in which bright, communicative, talented, and wonderful kids have every ounce of motivation and spirit drained out of them because we tolerate unthinking bullies in the classroom. I'm sufficiently bothered by what you have described to me that I would happily speak to the principal or superintendent in your school system if you wish to invite them to call me.

I'll address the specific issues you raised, but in this case, the matter is far more than a grading issue. This is about respect for children, and that, I fear, I cannot teach in a book.

First, I *do* agree that students should learn good writing skills, and I am also a stickler for the elements of correct grammar, spelling, and punctuation. But I have learned that with students of any age, from my second graders, who write wonderful stories for our school newspaper, to my 55-year-old graduate students, who are distinctly less creative, I do not get great results through humiliation. Writing is important, and accurate spelling, punctuation, and grammar are important—the only question is how we can best achieve those goals.

Most writing teachers will tell you that great writing is all about rewriting. As novelist Stephen King once said, "To write is human, to edit is divine." We should *not* expect perfection the first time, but rather should expect students to see writing as a process that involves writing several drafts, soliciting feedback, and creating work products that grow in complexity, length, and personal meaning.

When it comes to editing, I've found that the best way to help children learn lessons of spelling, grammar, and punctuation is to ask questions, not issue commands or letter grades. I just tell them the truth: "I didn't understand this sentence—would you please read it to me?" Sometimes the very act of reading their work aloud will help students find their own mistakes. If that doesn't work, *I'll* read it aloud—reading precisely what I see (not necessarily what they intended), and then they will hear the mistake and have the opportunity to correct it. If our objective is to give children the ability to independently write and complete work at increasingly advanced levels, then they must develop confidence in the process of writing, self-assessment, getting feedback from others, and then continuously improving their writing.

Finally, on the issue of scoring, the idea of using a percentage on a writing assignment is preposterous. State-of-the-art writing assessments typically have four or five levels, such as exemplary, proficient, progressing, and not meeting standards. At the elementary level, I have seen teachers use labels such as "Wow!," followed by "Good," followed by "Almost there," or other words that resonate with students. The key to these grading systems is that writing is a continuous process, not a one-shot evaluation.

I'm fully aware of the rejoinders this teacher might have: "He needs to learn to do it right the first time" and "We coddle kids too much these days." With regard to the first statement, I would only refer the teacher to your state writing standards. I assure you that they do not require proficient students to write quickly and perfectly on the first attempt. Indeed, most state standards explicitly refer to editing, revision, and the writing process. With regard to the issue of coddling, in more than three decades of leadership and teaching, I have not yet seen the adult or child who suffers from too much respect and love. The best teachers combine those qualities with exceptionally high expectations and achieve both great student work and emotionally healthy students.

If you do not have the option of changing teachers, schools, or districts, then I would certainly use this as an opportunity to let your son know that just as there are some kids in the world who haven't learned how to play well with others, there are also some adults who have yet to learn those lessons. I would also give him the opportunity to write at home and decorate a refrigerator door or wall or entire gallery with his writing, so that he knows that you know that he is a wonderful writer who is getting better every day. My book *Reason to Write* might be useful as well—it's just a small paperback with one version for students and another for parents.

We have made great strides in modifying our high school and district grading practices by eliminating zeros; limiting the impact of homework to ten percent of each quarter grade; utilizing "I" (to represent that a project is "in progress" and the student is working on it) and "N" (to represent that a project is incomplete and the student is not working on it) when major assignments are not turned in or are below standard; and providing a systematic pyramid of intervention. It's still an uphill battle with some teachers and parents, but I believe I have the full support of the superintendent and most board of education members. Furthermore, I am absolutely convinced (thanks to you) that grading students against a standard, not against one another, is a fairness issue and a value we must uphold as educational leaders. I am also convinced that it will take one teacher at a time, one school at a time, and one district at a time to change a 100-year tradition. I'm up for the challenge of doing my part to make that happen.

As we continue to transform our culture, I seek your advice. I am not comfortable with our guidelines that state that if a student misses a midterm or final exam, he or she fails the class. What is your position on final exams? What role should they play in a standards-based system? How should we deal with the student who "blows off" the exam at the end of a course when we have eliminated the option of averaging a zero into the final grade?

 Here are a few thoughts about midterms and finals:

First, any "one-shot" assessment, including final exams, encourages disrespect for teacher feedback. Such assessments take an enormous amount of time for teachers to evaluate, yet yield nothing in terms of impact on students. If you must have final exams, then I'd rather follow the example of Joel McKinney, a principal in Indianapolis whose ninth grade science pass rate zoomed from 36 percent to 69 percent to 92 percent, largely because he moved the "final" up two weeks earlier in the schedule than the "official" final exams. If students, as you noted, "blow it off" then the penalty is not a failure, but doing it again. Contrary to popular belief, that does *not* encourage students to be lazy and put the work off. Rather, it encourages students to get it right the first time and earn two weeks of freedom. As Thomas Guskey and many other researchers have established, grading as punishment does not work. What students fear is not failure or a low grade, but more work. Therefore, the appropriate "punishment" for blowing off a final or mid-term is making them *do the work.*

Second, the time-bound nature of finals and midterms frequently encourages the least rigorous and revealing item format—multiple-choice. As I have written in the early chapters of *Making Standards Work*, multiple-choice items are not necessarily more "objective" than performance tasks, and they certainly reveal far less about student abilities than performance tasks. Districts such as yours should be seeking every opportunity to challenge students far beyond merely "meeting standards" and should develop opportunities for them to display exemplary performance. Despite their reputation for being difficult, midterms and finals tend to encourage short-term bursts of energy rather than intensive and fully developed thinking.

Third—let me just speak as a teacher—finals and midterms are the worst combination of lots of work for little reward. I don't mind staying up, working hard, and giving students my best efforts, as long as the result is better performance and improved learning. Efforts devoted to coaching, encouraging, demanding, and providing feedback result in better performance, which justifies my missing some weekend time. But spending the same hours grading papers that are never reviewed by students, never used to improve performance, and are simply an accounting drill used to establish a grade on the transcript—well, that's not worth losing a Sunday evening.

I understand that you have colleagues who believe that students need discipline, time management, and rules. I agree. But I am suggesting that the rituals of midterms and finals are less likely to achieve those desired results than a menu of rigorous performance tasks that are distributed throughout the class.

 During a recent presentation, you mentioned a predicted relationship between a student's grades and his or her state exam results. How is that predicted relationship determined? Is it teacher prediction, or is it something else?

 In brief, the "predicted" relationship was just a hypothesis—and not a very risky one at that. My hypothesis was that "Kids who get 'D's' and 'F's' are much more likely to flunk state exams than kids who get 'A's,' 'B's,' and 'C's.'" That was just common sense—or so I thought.

The actual relationship shows that "common sense" is pretty uncommon.

I always use this disclaimer: Although my research is pretty good, it might not fit your system. So do your *own* investigation—get a random sample of 30 or more students who failed the state exam, and then look at their grades. If you see some "A's," "B's," and "C's," then it is fair to ask how in the world students who can't pass basic literacy and math tests get such good grades.

My research is not intended to apply to every district—it just serves as a prompt for you to do your own investigation.

 I have a research question dealing with the high end of the grading spectrum: Some educators think that the highest letter grade should be an "A+" but others think it should be an "A." Do you have any information about the "A+" issue?

 Before we consider the "A" vs. "A+" controversy, there is a prior issue to consider, and that is the purpose of the distinction between those two grades. If the purpose is to reward one excellent student for "beating" another excellent student, then we have simply retreated to the bell curve, with all of its attendant problems. When grading becomes comparative, it not only punishes excellent students, but also perversely rewards mediocre students: "He didn't meet my standards, but he was the best kid in the class, so he gets a high grade." Think of what would happen if we applied this logic to driver's education, or classes with safety risks involving welding, electricity, or chemicals. We'd have a lot of lousy drivers and severely injured kids who "weren't as bad as the other kids," rather than students who are proficient and safe.

If the purpose of the "A+" is to create a distinct level of exemplary performance, defined up front and objectively (not after the fact and subjectively based on teacher hindsight), then I have no problem with it. Frankly, "A's" are way too cheap in most classes, and I would be happy to live with additional challenges for students at the "A+" level—but *only* if that really means an objective challenge in which it is possible for several students, or no students, to earn the grade based upon the clear achievement of an objective standard. Moreover, I would argue that the "A+" must not be a reward merely for fast work, or effortless brilliance, but rather must be a reward that comes from hard work, respecting teacher feedback, and making multiple attempts to achieve outstanding performance.

Are you aware of any hard research about the relationship between student achievement and displaying final student work samples?

It's certainly not merely the displays that matter, but rather how the displays are used. There is substantial research in my own work (including *The Daily Disciplines of Leadership, The Leader's Guide to Standards, Accountability for Learning,* and *Accountability in Action*), as well as by Kati Haycock and The Education Trust, Linda Darling-Hammond, and many others, that collaborative scoring of student work is a practice associated with improved achievement and equity. And even if there were not a single statistic supporting it, a professional practice supporting the moral imperative of fairness is probably a good idea.

When it comes to displays, they are most effective if they are exceptionally specific. For example, one of the most effective displays of student work I have seen included student work in the middle, and rubrics around the circumference of the work, and then specific parts of the student work were highlighted, and linked with yarn to specific parts of the rubric. You want to know what "transition" looks like? See this essay. Want to know what good "voice" is? See this phrase. Want to see good organization? Check out this essay. At the end of the day, it's what teachers and students *do* with displays that matters most.

I was in attendance at a presentation in which you referenced a study having to do with female students receiving higher grades resulting from cooperative behavior or compliance, rather than demonstrated performance. I would like to read that study. Can you direct me to it?

My study of grades is included in *The Learning Leader.*

I have to confess, however, that my research is not particularly new or striking, but simply confirms what other researchers, such as Thomas Guskey, have been saying for many years. Guskey has written extensively on the subject, but if you'd like something that is focused explicitly on high schools, I recommend his article in the December 2000 issue of *The NASSP Bulletin,* "Grading Policies that Work Against Standards...and How to Fix Them." My article in the December 2004 issue of *Kappan,* "The Case Against the Zero," might also be of interest.

The superintendent for my school has shared your "Top Ten Things High Schools Can Do to Improve Achievement Now" (www.leadandlearn.com/hs-tips) with our counseling and administrative staff. We are interested in gathering more information that we hope to apply to our school.

Is this program being utilized in any schools our size and make-up (500 students in grades 7–12, with a traditional schedule)?

 My "Top Ten" list is certainly not a "program"—it's just a list of very specific professional practices I and my colleagues have observed in successful schools. The documentation of case studies for these schools appears in a variety of places, including my books *Accountability in Action* and *Accountability for Learning;* my article "Preventing 1,000 Failures" that appeared in the November 2006 issue of *Educational Leadership;* and *On Common Ground* (DuFour, Eaker, & DuFour, 2005) See also case studies published by the National Association of Secondary School Principals Bulletin (www.principals.org), the American Association of School Administrators (www.aasa.org), and the ASCD (formerly the Association for Supervision and Curriculum Development) publication *Educational Leadership* (www.ascd.org).

You might want to consider first conducting a needs analysis of your own school, including not only what the student needs are, but what the faculty and staff perceive to be the relative costs (emotional, time, and financial) of changing things compared to the costs of remaining the same. If the number of graduating seniors equals the number of incoming freshmen, if the morale of the faculty is sky-high, if students of all backgrounds have equal opportunities for success, if there is, in brief, no risk in remaining the same, then there isn't much reason to consider my "Top Ten" list.

But most schools we work with find that there are very significant costs—emotional and financial—of remaining the same. Once schools acknowledge that is true, then they can say, "Even if Reeves is completely crazy, what do we have to lose by trying some of these ideas? What is the risk of improving our schedule and grading system? What is the risk of communicating more effectively with parents, students, and colleagues? Even if we're wrong, will we be any worse off than we are now?"

I try pretty hard to avoid making grandiose claims. I've never claimed to have made the silver bullets that will solve schools' problems, and certainly do not claim to have created a proprietary program that schools must purchase in order to discover the "secret" of school improvement.

Consider a pilot program in your *own* school. Let each department or grade level implement just one or two of the ideas. Try a semester without zeroes, with multiple opportunities for exams, or with an early final exam. Treat it like a science project—express a hypothesis, gather data, and report the results. Some will work; others won't; others will have mixed results. That's the life of educational research, and we should welcome that complexity. Most of all, I hope that you and your colleagues will conclude that it's *your* "Top Ten" list, and not mine.

Q 88   **I like the idea of displaying student work, but I teach in a native community, and many students' grades are poor. I often don't show students each other's grades. How can I display work that is less than satisfactory, to avoid having work from the same students displayed over and over again?**

A   My advice is to post *exemplary* student work without the names of the students attached. To avoid social conflict among students and parents, you might consider exchanging work with teachers in other schools, so that you can say with integrity, "This is the quality of work I expect at the highest level, and this is the quality I will not accept, at the lowest level—but to avoid embarrassing anyone, I promise you that none of these work samples are from our community—they are all anonymous work samples from other communities that are similar to ours."

Another idea is that you do not post the *first* piece of work that students submit, but rather their *best* pieces of work. Marie's first piece of work might be exemplary, but the best work by Douglas might be his ninth submission. Douglas is learning more slowly, but he is persistent, and his ninth attempt at an assignment—if it meets your standards of excellence—deserves a place of honor as surely as Marie's first attempt.

CHAPTER 6

90/90/90

90/90/90

As a staff, we have reviewed the success of the schools represented in your article: "High Performance in High Poverty Schools: 90/90/90 and Beyond." There are several teachers who would like to take a research trip to visit locations and experience what one or more of these schools do on a day to day basis.

The 90/90/90 schools—schools with 90 percent poverty, 90 percent minorities, and in which 90 percent of students achieve state standards—are using some great educational techniques. I've found that schools that have made gains are quite open to sharing their ideas, and I will be happy to provide you with information about such schools in your area, but I'd like to add this caution: In my long-term research on high-poverty, high-success schools, I have personally witnessed people come to these schools by the busload. They watch what the schools do, and observe their performance, but very, very rarely do people change their opinions. Those who believed that it was possible to have high success in a high poverty environment said, "I told you so!" and those who believed it was impossible said, "But see—*this* school and these *students* are different from ours, so it's still impossible for us to do this."

At the end of the day, the visits are OK, but they are not a replacement for the basics—spending time at faculty meetings doing collaborative scoring; creating common assessments with frequent and immediate feedback; changing the schedule to provide more time for literacy (three hours for elementary school; double blocks for middle and high school); limiting curriculum choice so that students are not allowed to choose to fail; changing report cards to give honest feedback to students. These are just a few of the things that successful schools do. If a visit will help people do this, then it's a great idea. But have an open discussion with the faculty about these issues before the visit.

I am a high school math teacher. I am interested in the data and methodology used in the 1995-1998 four-year study that was done on 90/90/90 schools.

I was the author of the original 90/90/90 studies, which you can download at www.LeadandLearn.com. I have updated that research in two books, *Accountability for Learning* and *Accountability in Action.* You should also consider the work of other researchers in the same field, including The Education Trust, which lists high-performing, high-poverty schools on its Web site (www.EdTrust.org). The Kentucky and California Departments of Education have similar sites.

All of that said, I want to offer this observation: The most effective practices of high poverty and high minority schools are stunningly similar to the most effective practices of schools which rich white kids attend—high standards, high expectations, frequent common assessments, multiple opportunities for success, and a focus on nonfiction writing. That's not 90/90/90 education, it's just good education.

When you refer to "ethnic minorities" in your research, exactly what do you mean? In our area, we have a substantial English Language Learner population. We are trying to determine if the composition of our school is similar to those in your studies about 90/90/90 schools.

Our research on high performance in high-poverty schools includes schools that are remarkably diverse ethnically and linguistically. Some schools, in fact, were 100 percent English as a Second Language (ESL) students. Although Spanish is the predominant home language, our studies included districts with more than forty different primary languages. What is interesting to me is that the hallmarks of these successful schools do not change, even as the characteristics of students change dramatically. For example, both the high- and low-poverty, high- and low-minority, and high- and low- ESL schools all tended to allocate significantly more time for literacy (three hours in the elementary schools, and double periods in secondary schools), offered multiple opportunities for student success on papers, homework, projects, and tests, provided a laser-like focus on achievement, with recognition of student work in trophy cases and "walls of fame," and uniformly had very large doses of nonfiction writing in virtually every class, not just in language arts classes.

For specific high school case studies, you might want to look at my books *Accountability for Learning* and *Accountability in Action.*

 92

What are the names of the elementary schools in California that are 90/90/90 and are achieving above 850 on California's Academic Performance Index? Are there any schools in the nation that have an English Language Learner population higher than 70 percent that are scoring at about the 80th percentile on standardized tests?

You can find California schools that fit the high-performing, high-poverty criteria at www.springboardschools.org. You can also find them at www.EdTrust.org in the "Dispelling the Myth" section.

With regard to the English Language Learner question, I recommend that you talk to Earl Shore of Mead Valley Elementary School in Riverside County (Reeves, 2009b), one of several schools with 100 percent ELL and poverty students that have made consistent gains over the past four years.

Finally, I want to note that the criteria for 90/90/90 schools is not 90th percentile, but rather that 90 percent of students meet or exceed state standards. You can find additional details in my books *Accountability for Learning* and *Accountability in Action.* In addition, there are free downloadable study guides and newsletters at.www.LeadandLearn.com.

It's reasonable to set high expectations for the achievement of state standards for schools, including schools with a high percentage of students who do not speak English at home and whose parents have low incomes. It is not reasonable, however, to say that high standards are equal to the 80th percentile. The very essence of standards is not that one student is better than another, but rather that students achieve a standard that is accessible to all students with sufficient time and work.

93

The new principal at our school has just begun introducing us to the characteristics of 90/90/90 schools and the research you have done on them. However, the only aspect that she is focusing on is writing. There is no support for children who are not able to perform at grade level. There is no school-wide or community-wide focus on achievement. In other words, achievement is not celebrated in any way.

I teach release-time science, which means that students come to me for three periods per week, 45 minutes per period. In the 90/90/90 work that I read, you wrote that if children have good literacy teaching (three hours per day), scores in science, social studies and math rise, even though the teaching time in those subjects may be reduced due to literacy teaching. My questions are: Should the way science is taught (hands-on learning, supported by textbook, videos, and class discussion) change? Should the science teacher teach literacy through the science text? In other words, should the science teacher be teaching literacy lessons, but just using science content rather than novels, poetry, or whatever might be selected during language arts?

I interpreted your results to mean that with good literacy teaching in the language arts subjects, results on science tests improved because students could read and understand the content better during science instruction as well as on standardized science tests.

I guess I am frustrated because my principal is forcing me to teach literacy during science and that, to me, is very different from teaching science. Also, scientific writing (keeping good notes, writing up the results of experiments, analyzing and drawing conclusions from what you did during an experiment, etc.) is different from summarizing the content in a textbook. It is a skill that is not usually taught within other curricular disciplines and is essential to learn to be successful as a scientist and to train organized, sequential, critical thinking. If I teach literacy *and* scientific writing, I have time for nothing else, so my students end up learning next to no science.

Please clarify for me what science instruction might look like at a 90/90/90 school.

I'll be happy to share examples of what I have seen as effective science instruction in schools that are seeking to improve student literacy skills and also help students develop an interest in science.

It certainly is true that literacy is the primary skill not only for science, but also for every other subject. If students can't read the textbooks, lab procedures, or instrument markings, then they will not be successful in science. But the emphasis on literacy certainly does not exclude the possibility of a successful science program. Examples of specific techniques I've observed include:

1. Science "word walls" are created so that students learn scientific vocabulary that is appropriate to their grade level. I have particularly seen this technique in Norfolk, Virginia, where the science tests at the elementary and middle schools require sophisticated vocabulary. The word walls give teachers and students the opportunity to use science vocabulary in sentences in a variety of contexts. In other words, they not only incorporate literacy into science instruction, but they also incorporate science vocabulary into literacy instruction.

2. Labs specifically incorporate strong literacy skills, including writing scientific questions, writing predictions and hypotheses, writing observations in complete sentences, writing inferences from the graphs and charts used to collect data, and, of course, writing the conclusions. I think it is particularly important that, even when students work in a group on a lab project, each individual student is responsible for the lab log and the other writing described above.

3. Science projects are integrated with other subjects. I've seen examples of cooperation between physical education and science, for example, when students recorded VO2 (oxygen consumption) data from exercising students in gym class as part of a biology unit. Students have done wonderful projects in art using color combinations as part of a light and color unit in science. The opportunities for collaboration abound.

Finally, I do think it's important to note that in almost every state, the science curriculum has too many discrete objectives to be covered in the amount of time most teachers have. The answer for this is not for students and teachers to race through the curriculum in the hope that coverage will lead to learning. A better approach is using Power Standards (see Larry Ainsworth's book *Power*

Standards) so that teachers in different grades collaboratively select the most important standards and ensure that students become proficient in those standards rather than being exposed to a large variety of standards but becoming proficient at very few of them.

With regard to the "hands-on" question, it's an interesting quandary. I'll bet that you have seen the same thing I have—some absolutely wonderful hands-on units, full of inferential reasoning, genuine discovery, and solid scientific connections. And we've also seen hands-on units that have four kids watching aimlessly while one kid does the work, or kids diligently involved in an exciting hands-on unit involving content that has nothing to do with required student learning. So it's difficult to say that hands-on is always good or always bad—it's all about the quality of the instruction and engagement of the students. Dr. Michael Klentschy and colleagues did a very interesting National Science Foundation study (2000) which linked student writing and hands-on units to success on state multiple-choice tests.

One final thing—my 90/90/90 writings are not a "system"—just a set of observations Nonfiction writing is quite important, but so are the other elements—collaborative scoring among teachers, multiple opportunities for students to learn, and a relentless focus on student achievement, including, as you suggest, celebration. I've been in schools where exemplary science work is in the trophy case, along with athletic trophies, great student writing, wonderful artwork, and superior social studies projects.

I'm looking for a mixed-methods study on education or language acquisition. Is the 90/90/90 study from your book *Accountability in Action* a mixed-methods study?

If by "mixed-methods" you mean a combination of quantitative research (analysis of test scores), and qualitative research (observations, interviews, and narrative evaluation), then yes, the 90/90/90 study is certainly a mixed-methods study.

However, I would never rely upon a single study for inferences. We are continually updating and revising our findings. For example, one of the key 90/90/90 findings was the relationship between nonfiction writing and improved student achievement in other areas. We followed that up with a large-scale quantitative analysis of the relationship between increased student writing and improvements in math, science, and social studies (see my book *The Daily Disciplines of Leadership*). Later, we integrated those findings with more observational research (see my book *Accountability for Learning*).

Therefore, when you consider "mixed-methods" research, please do not consider an individual study in isolation, but rather consider the totality of research in the field. I think that educators and leaders are best served by the intersection of multiple methods. For example, with regard to the writing example in the previous paragraph, an important new contribution is a meta-analysis by Steve Graham and Dolores Perin in the August 2007 issue of the *Journal of Educational Psychology* that nicely complements the quantitative and qualitative research to which I have referred. Each study I've done is just one tiny pebble on the mountain of research. It is the sum of the work of many researchers working from different perspectives that will be most constructive for our profession.

 I am the principal of a school that has a vision of helping my school become another 90/90/90 school. I just surveyed my staff regarding what they think causes student achievement, and, sadly, their answers still largely reflect external factors, such as parent involvement. I, like you, spend much time away from my own children trying to figure out how to ensure success for 715 children whom I didn't bear, but whom I care for deeply. I refuse to believe that our school community contains an over-representation of learning-handicapped students. What actions do you suggest I take to help my staff accept personal accountability for the learning of our students?

 My best suggestion is that you create a "Science Fair" for teachers. Details about such "Science Fairs" are available in my book *Reframing Teacher Leadership to Improve Your School*. This will help you highlight the most effective practices among your colleagues. With more than 700 students, I'm confident that you have "islands of excellence," and your challenge as a leader is to identify, document, and replicate these extraordinary teaching and learning experiences.

For those who do not believe that 90/90/90 success is possible, my words will not be nearly as persuasive as the documentation of your colleagues.

How have the 90/90/90 schools managed the time issue—time needed for instruction in core content vs. additional time needed for interventions?

How have these schools formed relationships with each child in such a way that they all feel connected to the school community? Is a common homeroom, where each teacher is responsible to a few students as their mentor, counselor, coach, etc. a viable option?

90/90/90 schools typically spend *much* more time on literacy—180 minutes per day is not unusual—for *every* student, not just those in need of intervention. They still find time for science, social studies, music, and art, but not every subject receives the same amount of time. Literacy comes first, and it is "sacred time." For more elaboration on elementary and secondary schools where this is working, please see my 2009 book *Leading Change in Your School*.

You are quite right about the importance of relationships. While schools use different approaches, including homerooms, academic advisories, service learning, student-led peer groups, or formal multi-year advisor-student relationships, they all have this in common: relationships are not left to chance. Time in these sessions is *structured*, not just an extra study hall or informal babysitting. In the best cases, the relationship leader knows which students need assistance, and they quickly get down to business: "You missed a couple of algebra assignments last week—what can we do right now to get this corrected?" "It looks as if you're having some trouble understanding last week's science assignment—let's take a look at it right now and see if you and one of your classmates can work it out." "You had a confrontation with some other kids yesterday—let's talk about how to deal with conflict, and first, I'd like to hear your side of the matter."

How does this work in practice? There must be *great* communication from teachers to counselors, who, in turn, communicate priority student issues to the faculty members and administrators who are leading these relationship groups. The key is providing *immediate* support and intervention, not a "program for failing students" after it's too late.

CHAPTER 7

Accountability

Accountability

I have found your thoughts on islands of excellence and systemic change to be very helpful, along with Stephen Covey's *The 8th Habit*. In that book, Covey appears to make a very clear distinction between accountability based on results and accountability based on method. He basically says that when accountability is based on results, people are empowered and performance goes up. However, when it is based on method, people are disempowered and performance will be lower. I have applied this principle in my district, and have seen teachers respond in ways that far exceeded my expectations.

For example, four years ago, 33 percent of our first-grade students left first grade reading clearly below grade level, and 17 percent were "approaching" grade level, according to our end-of-the-year assessments. As I met with the team, I talked with them a lot about the results and how to improve student learning, but stayed away from insisting on a particular fix. They were as disturbed by the results as I was. That summer, they went away as a team and studied *On Solid Ground*, by Sharon Taberski and Shelley Harwayne, and significantly revamped their instruction. The results have been very gratifying—each year since, the number of students leaving first grade reading below grade level has declined. This past year, only 3 percent of first-graders left reading clearly below grade level, and another 16 percent approaching grade level. The rest were at or above the standard, with 29 percent reading above grade level.

I have observed similar results with other teams in the building over and over again. When they are empowered, teachers consistently use their creativity to improve student learning far above what I would have predicted. And yet I still see much in the educational leadership literature that seems to promote dictating method and emphasizing accountability based on method of instruction rather than based on results. What are your thoughts?

I, too, appreciate Covey's work, but I don't think either of us would paint the dichotomy between results and methods quite so starkly. Clearly you are correct that results must be our focus, but we dare not ignore *how* those results are achieved. For example, the fastest way to increase average test scores is to increase the dropout rate among disadvantaged and/or English as a Second Language children. Similarly, the fastest way to lose weight might be drug abuse and eating disorders, but we would use those "methods" at our peril, and they do not result in long-term sustainable improvements. Moreover, as your own example indicates, you did pay attention to methods *and* results—and that led to what sounds like a great example of professional learning associated with improved results.

My concern when someone says, "As long as I'm getting results, I don't worry about how I get them," is that it can then be difficult or impossible to replicate those good results. In a learning community, we need both results and methods. Finally, when teachers are in schools that are in transient communities, with a lot of student turn-over, a focus on results for students they did not even teach for most of the year can be de-motivating, and ruinous to their professional lives.

 We follow the Professional Learning Communities (PLC) format in our school district. Teams have fifty minutes of PLC time each week. One of my fifth-grade teachers came to me today and expressed her frustration with her teammates. Two of her teammates do not contribute well or understand the dynamics of analyzing student data. This teacher doesn't want to meet with them, because she feels they are holding her back. I support her decision to collaborate with other teachers, but I am concerned the other teachers on her team will be left out. How do you suggest I proceed to ensure equitable learning opportunities for all students?

While I don't know the details of this particular situation, I can tell you that mutual frustration on these matters is not unusual. Some teachers are enthusiastic about the possibilities of PLCs and data analysis, and other teachers find it a futile waste of time. Before you give up on that team, I'd like to suggest some alternatives.

First, ask the teammates who are unwilling to cooperate to express their core needs. "What would be necessary in order for you to believe that your PLC time is well spent?" If the answer is, "nothing," then it's a pretty clear signal that you need to provide additional duties for them. But I think most teachers will say, "Look—we're just frustrated because we find that a lot of what administrators label as 'collaboration' just doesn't go anywhere. We want to help kids, but we are tired of wasting time. Please give us some clear direction and purpose, and then we can cooperate."

Give your colleagues the benefit of the doubt. Assume that they just want some clear direction and purpose, and that it's up to you, as the leader, to provide that. Consider some very specific scenarios for data analysis. The teachers should review the data, find students with specific needs, and then recommend a specific course of action. Those actions might involve pull-outs, centers, reassignment of teachers or classes, or a change in schedule. And then support their recommendations. If a leader asks teachers for advice and opinions, it is essential that the leader provide a good faith indication that their opinions will lead to action.

Second, give the teammates specific responsibility. If they are frustrated about parent involvement, student engagement, homework compliance, or behavior, then give them *very specific* opportunities to try new strategies to solve those problems. Have them experiment with alternatives and report the results to their colleagues.

Third, plan to celebrate some small wins. For both the teacher who is showing leadership and for those teachers who are expressing reservations, it is imperative that they hear not just rhetoric and promises, but some real results. This does not need to be grand-scale: "This year's state test scores are 25 percent better than last year's test scores." Rather, you can provide data on a short-term impact: "This month, we had levels of homework compliance and positive student behavior that were 25 percent better than the same month last year." Think of what you can do right now—this month—to motivate your colleagues, your students, and yourself.

For the past ten years, I have been working on school improvement and improved student achievement. Now I am putting together the information from all of the books I have read and workshops I have attended, etc. to formulate a few essential questions. I have worked with a variety of school leaders, from superintendents of districts, to site principals, to county staff, to state staff, etc., and I feel that few of them completely understand the big picture. I have listened to you speak, read your books, and attended your trainings, and I feel that you *do* understand the big picture, so I would greatly appreciate your opinion about my thinking on these matters.

I have attended, read, listened to, and implemented dozens of trainings, programs, ideas, and reform initiatives, and it has finally occurred to me that while all of these methods may yield results, having a strong accountability system is a must. I think we must:

1. Determine explicitly, for each learning organization, what we truly want students to know and be able to do.

2. Set up assessments that determine accurately whether or not students know and are able to do those things.

3. Have a plan to address the situation if we are not getting the results we want.

Isn't it only after you have done those three things that you would know what to do next? Rather than providing professional development on differentiated instruction, direct instruction, cooperative learning, standards-based calibration, multiple-intelligences, higher-level questioning, English Language Learner strategies, use of technology, etc., based on hunches or the latest trends in improvement, shouldn't we tie those strategies to what we want students to actually be able to do and whether or not they are able to do it?

I work at a county office, and I am supposed to help districts foster school improvement, particularly in the area of schools targeted for Program Improvement under the No Child Left Behind Act. I want to steer them in the direction of building a strong foundational accountability system first, then move on to the specific needs they have. Am I heading in the right direction? I often feel that schools simply want me to help them fix the short-term problem—the achievement of English Language Learners or special education students, meeting state targets, etc.—without attempting to fix the bigger picture.

I share your frustration with the multiplicity of professional development alternatives, some of which can be unfocused and not directly related to the needs of students and teachers.

I would counsel against an "either/or" approach, that being to either focus on student learning needs as expressed in academic standards or to focus on effective teaching strategies. In fact, we must do both. You are quite right that we need to identify what students need to learn—that's what the academic content standards imposed by many states in the 1990s were all about, and nearly twenty years later, educators are still struggling with the issue. Perhaps the "answer" is that we need a 400-day school year. Therefore, we are still asking, "What do students need to learn?" The assessment data from annual testing provides feedback that is late and ineffective. That is why, of course, simply answering the questions you pose is not enough—the state thinks that those questions have already been asked and answered. We need effective teaching and assessment strategies, including, for example, Power Standards, and other issues I've addressed. There is great value to focusing on what is effective, and I don't suggest implementing a revolving door of professional development programs. But I will tell you that having standards is not enough.

You are right about the necessity of developing an accountability system. But most accountability systems are nothing more than a litany of test scores. You must insist on accountability not just for kids, but also for leaders, policy makers, teachers, parents, and communities. That is the "holistic" accountability I've written about and implemented in several districts across the country.

I attended your workshop on *Transforming Our Schools through Collaborative Professional Learning,* and it was outstanding. Can you provide me with ten bulleted points on Professional Learning

Communities that I can share with other educators to try to get them on board with establishing PLCs in their schools?

 Here are my thoughts about what real Professional Learning Communities do:

1. Real PLCs don't adjourn a meeting without a specific commitment to improved teaching practices.

2. Real PLCs hold administrators and teachers as accountable as students.

3. Real PLCs know the differences between opinion, personal experience, and evidence.

4. Real PLCs have evidence of improved student results that are a direct consequence of PLC decisions.

5. Real PLCs operate not because of administrative mandates, but because it's the right thing to do.

6. Real PLCs don't wait for the official "PLC Meeting"—they collaborate like they breathe, as a natural part of their day.

7. Real PLCs talk about their mistakes. The most senior teacher-leaders and administrative leaders in the PLC must talk about their own mistakes to create a safe environment to analyze experience and learn from it.

8. Real PLCs celebrate success—not just gains in annual test scores, but daily, weekly, and monthly improvements in teaching and learning.

9. Real PLCs encourage the discouraged teacher and student and challenge the complacent teacher and student.

10. Real PLCs are the most engaging, professional, rewarding, fun, and meaningful environment for those of us lucky enough to be teachers and educational leaders.

 I am interested in your theories about motivating teachers by showing them their progress. Is there an article about how a teacher can use a checklist of teaching improvement goals to see self-improvement, or does teacher motivation stem primarily from students' progress?

I think teachers need to see gains both in student achievement and in teacher progress. In my books *The Learning Leader* (2006) and *Accountability for Learning* (2004) I describe examples of how teachers can measure effective practice and identify progress. One method that a team of teachers can consider is measuring the percentage of their agreement when scoring anonymous samples of student work. The more clear and consistent their rubrics, the higher the percentage of agreement. Progress can also be measured in other key areas, such as the frequency of feedback to students and indicators that students use teacher feedback to improve the quality of their work.

For more information about motivational issues—for teachers, students, and all of us—I recommend Daniel Pink's book *Drive*. It's an excellent synthesis of the research about creating intrinsic motivation.

I am interested in how my district can make the best use of educational resources and time. I see two clear directions: developing a relevant, meaningful, and manageable curriculum, and creating an environment for learning in every classroom. How can we address both of these issues effectively without overwhelming teachers?

The things that matter most in achieving educational success are teaching, time, and leadership.

While I agree that curriculum and environment are important, I have worked in many districts that have invested a great deal of money and time in creating a magnificent curriculum, but they are not willing to give teachers the *time* that is required to deliver it. This error bears directly on your concern that we are overwhelming teachers. When I ask teachers around the world what they need, it is rare that they say that they need more curriculum, more resources, or even more money. They need *time.* Just today, I read a letter from an administrator who was ever so proud of his new literacy program that was full of demands and non-negotiable requirements for teachers. Yet he was providing the same number of minutes each day to the teachers who are expected to deliver that new program as he provided ten years ago.

In addition to *time*, the second thing that matters most is *teaching*. An article in *Educational Leadership* (Patterson, 2005) contains a compelling yet old story—the newest and least experienced teachers are assigned to the most challenging and difficult students. This creates a toxic cycle, in which those students are angry, cynical, bored, and failing; the teachers are similarly angry, cynical, bored, and failing. As the students quit, the school gains a worse reputation; as the teachers quit and new ones are brought in, their replacements are assigned to the least desirable schools in the district—the ones with the highest failure rates—and the cycle continues. We must make teaching our most challenging students a valuable and valued enterprise, and that is not a concept that tradition and contracts allow.

The third thing that matters most is *leadership*. We talk a good game about our education leaders taking responsibility for instruction and learning, but they are most frequently evaluated for their popularity and political skills. Therefore, when there is an opportunity to make a profoundly important change in something that will reduce failures and improve success, such as changing grading policies, more often than not, educational administrators will carefully consider the evidence that improved grading policies will reduce failures and improve student success, and then do ... *nothing*. Why? Because such changes are not popular with teachers, parents, and the public.

School administrators have mortgage payments to make and kids to send to college, and their economic incentives are almost entirely focused on political popularity rather than on making decisions that will improve achievement. In the short term, complaints beat reform almost every time.

In short, the best ways to make the most of educational time and resources are:

Time: Double or triple the amount of time devoted to literacy. Require every class—without a single exception—to include a nonfiction writing assessment at least once each quarter.

Teaching: Assign the very best teachers to the most challenging classes, and give them a combination of economic and noneconomic incentives (more time, lower class size, extra professional learning opportunities) to take on this challenge.

Leadership: Defend and support leaders who elevate

effectiveness over popularity. Terminate leaders who relish complacency, praying for different results next year even as they institutionalize the processes, procedures, and policies of last year.

My elementary school is in the beginning stages of adopting Professional Learning Communities. We have agreed to bank time, and to have at least one day per week next year to help facilitate PLCs. However, there are some practices occurring at my school that concern me that are being promoted as being part of PLCs. I have not had much PLC training, but I feel these practices do not follow the PLC philosophy. For example, we have three first-grade classes of twenty students each, and they are grouping students by ability and rotating the students for two and a half hours out of the school day. School begins at 8:15 a.m. They ability-group the students for language arts (high, medium, low), with one teacher instructing each group. This goes on from 8:25 a.m. to 10 a.m. every day. They group for math, in a similar manner, in the afternoon for an hour. This is also happening at other grade levels, though not to this extent. Personally, and philosophically, I greatly disagree with this practice. Our principal, however, is in favor of it, and is promoting this as part of PLCs. This seems to counter what PLCs are about. What is your opinion about this practice, and its relation to PLC methodology?

With regard to the primary question about whether PLCs and ability-grouping go hand in hand, I'd have to say that they are quite different matters. The essence of PLCs is a focus by teachers and administrators on meeting the needs of students. If a student needs help on skill-building, then it is appropriate to provide help to that student, in the same way that if the Celtics need work on shooting free-throws, it's entirely appropriate that those players get the extra practice that they need. The bigger issue, of course, is whether that is the *only* help that they need. No one would call a basketball practice complete if it *only* focused on the skill of shooting free-throws, and no literacy intervention is complete if it is only a two-and-a-half-hour phonics drill. The solution lies not in extremes, but in achieving balance. It can be quite appropriate to provide skill-based groupings for part of a class, and heterogeneous groupings to discuss, predict, and evaluate for the remainder of the class. Similarly, students in the orchestra and chorus have some parts of their class for sectional rehearsals and skill-building, but they all play or sing together for other parts of the rehearsal.

Finally, I would resist the notion that "because it is part of PLCs" is a sufficient justification for anything. The only reason to engage in a professional practice is that it is associated with helping students learn. The practices associated with PLCs can be part of that, but, as you have noted, the term PLC has been used by many people to represent many different things. So, as always, I would return to the real research, and also encourage action research at the school and classroom level, to identify the practices that are most effective for improving student performance in your school.

Q 104

Are there other schools besides the ones you mentioned in Norfolk, VA and Milwaukee, WI that have seen great success using your model for data collecting?

A

You can find examples all over the country. Here are some published sources for your consideration. My book *Accountability for Learning* includes case studies of elementary, middle, and high school data teams, and also includes specific examples of the use of our model. In addition, you can look at almost any issue of The Leadership and Learning Center magazine, back issues of which are available at www.LeadandLearn.com for examples of the application of data teams. But don't just settle for my work. Look at Michael Schmoker's excellent book *The Results Fieldbook* for case studies of data analysis. Also see Rick DuFour, Rebecca DuFour and Robert Eaker's *On Common Ground* to see a variety of researchers address the same issue. I would never claim that this is "my" system. It is a synthesis of the thinking of a lot of people, and each school ultimately must make it their own.

Q 105

I am a special education provider. There is much discussion about Response to Intervention and the use of this model with the Individuals with Disabilities Education Act (IDEA 2004). How do you see Response to Intervention and standards-based education

working together? Do you think that looking at the causes of achievement as well the effects in general education will, in any way, reduce the need for separate special education classes?

 The short answer is "yes"—there is clear cross-application between effective practices in special education and general education. I have frequently said that what most people call "special education" I would call "good education"—and we can all learn from one another.

Your question about causes and effects really gets to the heart of the issue. How can we best assess the causes of student achievement, not just effects? In general, I think that we must agree that as a moral principle, no child should be more accountable than the adults in the system. We have the ability to create scoring rubrics for special education and regular education teachers with regard to their implementation of differentiated instruction, effective assessment, accurate feedback, and other techniques we know to be effective. No accountability system is complete without an accurate and timely assessment of adult behavior.

CHAPTER 8

Leadership

Leadership

 We are evaluating whether or not to renew our superintendent's contract. Do you have any models for how to go about this process?

 First, the school board and superintendent should agree on the dimensions of leadership which are most important to meet the needs of your community. There are many models here—the Interstate School Leaders Licensure Consortium suggests twenty-four dimensions, my model suggests ten. Perhaps there is a middle ground that best meets your needs.

Second, define performance for each dimension along a continuum. Most superintendent evaluations unwisely use what can best be described as a mystical process in which each board member assigns a number, letter or description, and then the board chairperson says, "You are a 3.5 on a scale of 1 to 5"—but there is no clear definition of what a "4" or "5" really means. In my model, each level of performance is defined with a high degree of specificity.

Third, thoughtfully consider the implications for a leader who is *not* perfect in every dimension. The greatest flaw in most superintendent evaluations is the presumption of solitary leadership—once the person is hired, they must be superior in everything from technology to instructional leadership to budget management. The truth is that no one in the world meets this unrealistic requirement. What *is* reasonable is the expectation of the board that the superintendent will build a leadership *team* that can provide excellent performance in each area. Thus the superintendent might personally receive an evaluation that shows only adequate performance in a particular area, and that is not necessarily a negative, as long as the superintendent has recognized this weakness and created a leadership team that includes people who are better than he or she is in that area.

Ideally, these requirements are all made clear at the beginning of the relationship with the superintendent, and not when the decision is made to renew a contract. But you play the hand you are dealt. Whether you renew this contract or hire someone new, the next superintendent evaluation will be much more objective, fair, and reasonable for the board, community, and superintendent if the criteria for evaluation are established up front, and then when renewal time comes, the decision-making process is objective and transparent.

What interview questions would you ask a candidate for Superintendant of Schools? What questions would help determine the candidate's ability to be a relational leader?

I've elaborated on leadership evaluation in my book *Assessing Educational Leaders*, but let me offer some specific interview questions.

First, however, I want to note that there is a long history of a disconnection between the performance of prospective leaders in interviews and their actual behavior on the job. Therefore, the best (though certainly not failsafe) way to assess the candidates is to focus on specific situations that have actually occurred. Much of what happens in schools, particularly at the superintendent level, is public. A search of the candidate's local newspaper in the past year should be very informative about how he or she has dealt with school matters. This search will probably also suggest other people—education association leaders, parents, board members, community leaders, and students—who can be contacted to discuss a candidate's actual performance in his or her previous position.

Here are some questions I would ask of a prospective superintendent:

1. "Please provide very specific examples (without using real names, of course) of how you have confronted quality issues and resolved them. I would particularly like to know of a specific example dealing with quality improvement by a leader and one involving quality improvement by a teacher." The questioner may need to press on this to receive an appropriate answer. You are not asking for a Homeric epic on the value of quality or the leader's philosophy of quality—you are asking about how this person really addressed a specific quality problem. If he or she can't think of a specific example,

that may indicate that their prior district was 100 percent perfect, or may indicate that there were quality issues that he or she never confronted.

2. "Please provide a very specific example of an instance in which you did not win an argument or controversy with your boss—either a prior board or superintendent. What happened, and how did you resolve it?" The absence of controversy in a leader's life is not a good thing—beware of the leader who claims not to have had any, or who can only think of one controversy—the one that led him or her to apply for a position elsewhere.

3. "Please tell us, in detail, what you know about our district— our students, our teachers, our community, and our leadership. Based on this knowledge, please tell us two or three things that we could do to improve student achievement next year."

Finally, just to be fair, the board and interview committee should be ready to answer some questions themselves. If I were the superintendent candidate, here is what I would ask the board or interview committee:

1. "Why is my predecessor leaving? What specifically do you expect me to do differently from my predecessor?"

2. "Please provide an example of a parent complaint that has been made about a teacher and about an administrator in your district. How were those complaints handled? I am particularly interested in complaints that came to the board and how those complaints were handled." Many school boards will hire a superintendent, principal, or teacher with claims that they want higher academic achievement—and then will cave when there are parent complaints based on restricted student choices, extra student work, or unflattering student feedback.

3. "Please describe your expectations for the public visibility of the superintendent." It's a good idea to put implicit expectations on the table up front. If the failure of the superintendent to attend every athletic event, every performance, every assembly, and every board meeting; to

join the Rotary Club, hospital board, and Chamber of Commerce; and also to be in the office always available to take phone calls from every stakeholder is a firing offense, then don't expect any superintendent with a family or a life to take the job.

If you could ask only one question of a candidate interviewing for the position of high school principal, what would you ask?

My impulse is to say that the one question I would ask someone applying to be a high school principal these days would be "Are you *nuts?*"

But perhaps there is a better response. I actually would not ask a question; I would administer a performance assessment. Specifically, I would give the candidate a set of real data on two schools—one high-performing and one struggling. Obviously, the names of the schools, administrators, and teachers should be removed, but otherwise it should be authentic and complete data, with a fair amount of detail—classroom by classroom analysis, subgroup analysis, and subscale analysis. The question I would ask is this: "You've seen the data—what actions would you take as a leader?"

My experience suggests that the conversation will focus either on the characteristics of the students or on thoughtful and detailed actions that the leaders, teachers, and students must take to improve performance.

We are using the ideas you published in *The Learning Leader* with fifty of our local school leaders. A couple of times in the text, mention is made of a table of estimated instructional and leadership effectiveness coefficients to place on the horizontal axis of the "leadership map." Where can I find this table, or a list of these coefficients?

The quickest way to get a list of leadership factors is to visit www.LeadandLearn.com, and go to the survey for Leadership Maps. You don't have to purchase the map subscription—just look at the items, and you can see everything that we have taken into account in developing the map. We have determined that mere correlation coefficients were an insufficient basis on which to create an effective leadership map. People would claim, for example, to be "doing Professional Learning Communities" or "using Robert Marzano's strategies," both of which have high effectiveness coefficients *only if implemented properly*. Therefore, we changed the configuration of the Leadership Map to include "degree of implementation," rather than the correlation coefficient of the individual practice. Therefore, a highly effective (i.e., highly correlated to student achievement) practice will only receive a high score on the horizontal axis of the map if that practice is implemented at a high level.

Many of the school systems in our state are beginning the process of developing new leadership evaluation instruments for school leaders in a standards-based world. I am currently examining the new leadership performance standards that were recently approved by our Professional Standards Commission and the University System Board of Regents. These will be used with new leader preparation.

Some of my colleagues would like to develop a list of rubrics for these performance standards and to use these to evaluate principals. However, I am skeptical both of our ability to do this and of the appropriateness of using rubrics to judge such a complex job. Anything that we come up with will also have to pass legal scrutiny.

Do you know of anyone who has already done something similar to this and has developed an instrument that could be used by system leaders to evaluate building-level leaders? Or do you know of any resource that could help us?

My book *Assessing Educational Leaders* (2nd ed., 2008) contains precisely what you are asking for—a field-tested leadership evaluation rubric. I'd never claim it's a perfect instrument, but perhaps it could serve as a first draft, and save you and your colleagues a good deal of time.

The Leadership and Learning Center has worked with school systems, state education departments, and international organizations to create and improve leadership evaluation. Here are a couple of ideas you might want to consider:

1. Make this a cooperative effort with school boards. The weakest link in leadership evaluation has been superintendent evaluation, and the rubric approach that you suggest is particularly important when politics, rather than performance, can influence the picture. It is essential that school boards are part of the creation of this strategy, because they are likely to resist a "solution" that is imposed on them.

2. Distinguish performance coaching from evaluation. Some feedback, particularly that which will come from a detailed design such as our Leadership Performance Matrix, will inevitably lead to the conclusion that the leader is imperfect. This is a startling finding when one is accustomed to traditional evaluations, in which anything short of "superior" is a dagger in the heart. If you introduce a two-step process that starts not with matters influencing contract renewal or the ability to pay the mortgage, but rather with the broad question of "How can we help you to be a more effective leader?" then I think you'll have better results. Moreover, the inevitable tension between the state department of education and individual school systems can be mitigated if you treat the initial leadership evaluation not as a "gotcha!" but as a means to provide assistance.

3. Leave room for local nuance. While there are some constants of effective leadership, I've been to enough schools around the country to know that there are very different school systems and very different areas within the same state. A good system of leadership evaluation will recognize and respect local issues.

I have just finished reading *The Learning Leader* for a graduate class, and I'm not quite clear on how to plot the "X" axis of the Leadership Map using quantitative data. How does one assign a number in the range "-1" to "+1"? Since this is evaluating the effectiveness of teaching and leadership strategies, is the score more subjective? If not, how *would* I determine the value of the "X" axis?

The horizontal axis on the Leadership Map can represent one of two things—either the effectiveness of a teaching and leadership strategy, or the percentage of implementation of a strategy that you have already determined to be effective.

In the first case, effectiveness, the "X" value represents the correlation of the practice to improved achievement, ranging from −1.0 (perfectly ineffective) to +1.0 (consistently and perfectly effective). For example, the correlation between nonfiction writing and student achievement is about .8; the correlation between effective feedback and student achievement is about .6. Many authors (see most prominently Robert Marzano) have identified these relationships.

In the second case, implementation, the "X" value represents the percentage of implementation, ranging from 0 to 100 percent, with 50 at the midpoint. Therefore, if 5 percent of the faculty attend a conference and implement its strategies in the classroom, then that number is pretty far to the left side of the matrix—you only get to the "leading" and "learning" quadrants when a majority of faculty are implementing the strategy.

As always, I don't claim scientific certainty for these ideas—it's a way to conceptualize the relationships between student achievement and the work of teachers and leaders, not a sure-fire formula. Beware of people who claim to have the latter.

 I am a high school principal. I read your article "Preventing 1,000 Failures" in *Educational Leadership*. My high school is struggling with the implementation of the initiatives you mention in the article. There is not buy-in among the staff for these processes. We are currently doing balanced assessments, according to the model created by Rick Stiggins. I have attended your workshops on two occasions, and I took a group of educators to a Stiggins Assessment for Learning institute to start the process from the ground up. Teachers taught other teachers these practices for twelve months. We are continuing the process now with more training and talking, but the data indicate that educators are not buying into these strategies. And our data on grades is quite the opposite of those from the school mentioned in your article. We are experiencing what might be called an "implementation dip."

Our district has a strong interest in making this process work for kids. Please help us decide what to do next. We have the same strategies in place as the school mentioned in your article. The problem is staff buy-in. We have a focus group here that is desperate to get some good advice about how to handle this.

 Essentially, you are asking "What do we do when we're doing the right things but not getting results?" and "What do we do when we know the right thing to do and the staff still doesn't buy in?"

First, conduct some more inquiry about the details. For example, in one district we serve, administrators complained about a lack of teacher buy-in. But a review of actual practices showed that 16 percent of teachers were leading implementation efforts and another 53 percent were willing to model implementation, while 29 percent had limited implementation, and 2 percent had no implementation. That may not be great, but I had to challenge the principal and superintendent by saying, "How much time are you spending nurturing the 16 percent and 53 percent—the teachers who are doing all you ask—rather than arguing with the 29 percent and 2 percent?"

With regard to implementation, I also have to challenge teachers. When they say, "We're doing monthly integrated writing assessments" and I say, "Great—it's November, so I'd really like to see those assessments for September and October," sometimes they reply, "We'll, we really haven't quite started yet." There's a big difference between claims and realities for implementation. I'm also very skeptical when schools claim to be doing a lot of additional work, but there are no changes in the schedule. Last week, I heard a principal claim to have seven new literacy initiatives, but he had not expanded the literacy block by a single minute. In short, it's important to check the evidence behind claims and assumptions.

Second, I'm more than happy to admit I'm wrong. I call it the "Groucho School of Leadership," named after the old Groucho Marx comedy sketch: "Doctor! It hurts when I do *this*." And the doctor says, "Well, then, stop doing that." Think about football practice this week—I'm willing to bet that changes were made in practice based on observations made during last week's game. You should ask, "What are we going to do *differently* in December based on what we've learned so far?" Sometimes I'll find—particularly with assessment models from Rick Stiggins, myself, or any of us who advocate effective classroom assessments—that teachers had the right idea, but the wrong execution. For example, even a really engaging and effective classroom assessment loses its power if students do not receive feedback that is accurate and immediate. No matter who wrote the rubric for an assessment, it's worthless if, in practice, five teachers look at a piece of student work and come to five different opinions about student proficiency. Every strategy I advocate is just a hypothesis—and every teacher who objects to my ideas has a perfect right to do that—as long as they offer a better hypothesis and they are willing to test their hypothesis with evidence and prove me wrong. If they prove me wrong by coming up with better ways to improve student results, then that's the kind of failure I can easily live with.

Third, and most importantly, please examine the data on a classroom-by-classroom basis. I can tell you that in almost every district, the district or school averages don't tell the whole story. It's only when you examine individual classes or small groups that you find where improvement is—and is not—happening. What you are more likely to find is that when you implement particular strategies in particular ways, then you have gains. When you don't have that implementation, you don't have success. I'd consider conducting a "treasure hunt" at your school—using that exact terminology, so that the faculty knows your inquiry is a *treasure* hunt, not a *witch* hunt. Find and identify the exemplary practices that you can link to improvement.

In your book *Reframing Teacher Leadership to Improve Your School* (2008), you discuss starting a "best practices" book. I would like to try that idea, but I'm not entirely clear about what the one-page submission from each teacher would look like. Do you mean that each teacher should write about a best practice that they use and describe how they use it? Or do you mean that each teacher should provide a one-page lesson plan that incorporates a best practice tip?

The one-page best practice sheet should be very simple, perhaps with some questions to prompt teacher responses. Something like:

1. What was the challenge?

2. What did you do?

3. What were the results?

4. What are your "lessons learned" that you would be willing to share with your colleagues?

Ideally, every teacher can find some success story to share. By keeping it to one page, you avoid unintended competition among colleagues and you make the document accessible to everyone.

 I am constantly amazed at how little the school's central office is brought into the conversation of teaching and learning. How would you involve central office staff in such conversations? And why is so little research and writing being done about the role of the central office in education?

 You are absolutely right that the central office team is a critical part of school leadership. Fortunately, The Leadership and Learning Center has addressed this with two new research-based services devoted explicitly to the needs of central office leaders.

First, we have a senior leadership assessment, called *Hallmarks of Excellence*, designed for superintendents and central office leadership team members. This has been extensively evaluated, and I took it myself. Each assessment is completely confidential, and designed only to improve the performance of central office leaders, *not* for evaluation or public release. A personal leadership coach is assigned to each client to help interpret the results and develop a follow-up plan. As you know, many central office leaders attained their present position because they have had many years of superior evaluations. That's great—they are often terrific people—but good evaluations do not help them improve their leadership skills. The Hallmarks assessment does just that.

Second, we have a central office version of the Leadership Map, which allows central office colleagues to assess the relationship between their own actions and student achievement.

This week I attended the Leadership at Every Level Institute hosted by Solution Tree, at which you were a presenter. The way teacher leadership seemed to be presented throughout the Institute this week was to define it as "being a great teacher." The message seemed to be that teachers are not really leaders in the sense that they need to be taught leadership concepts and skills; they are leaders in the sense that they show the most expertise in doing their jobs well.

I think there is more to teacher leadership than that.

Often, teacher leaders are called upon to facilitate collaboration or marshal their teams to attack their work in an interdependent manner. I have found that teacher leaders often do not know how to do those things.

I know that principals should facilitate collaboration by setting parameters and guidelines for what the teams should do. But we cannot just throw people into a room and expect them to conquer the challenges of collaboration without assistance. And, we cannot ignore the fact that when teacher leaders enter a room full of hostile peers, they are facing a challenge, and they need support.

Teacher leaders need help with their leadership roles and are hungry for assistance in defining the roles, responsibilities, risks, and rewards of leadership. They need help with the part they play in building a positive school culture, dealing with negative team members, assisting the principal with vision-casting and communication, and other leadership skills.

As I look at the literature out there on teacher leadership, I feel like I am a lone voice advocating for something that no one else seems to find valuable, with the possible exception of Charlotte Danielson, who points out in her book *Teacher Leadership That Strengthens Professional Practice* that teacher leadership has not been well accepted.

What is your view of teacher leadership?

You are quite right that my definition of teacher leadership—impact on the professional practices of other teachers—is not at all the traditional view. There is a distinction between the team leadership role—and its attendant skills of agenda setting, project management, communication, political understandings, etc.—and the teacher leadership role. The former does, as you suggest, require *much* more leadership and management skills. But that doesn't make team leadership superior to teacher leadership—only different. One can be an effective teacher leader in my definitional scheme by effective modeling, action research, and sharing of best practices, even if one never leads a single meeting. The evidence I attempted to share suggests that this type of teacher leadership can be strikingly influential, even if it is not the traditional "teacher leader" by definition.

There are conflicts in the literature, and the researchers are not always consistent in their use of the term "teacher leadership." The same, of course, can be said of terms such as "Professional Learning Communities," a phrase that is used in wildly different ways by professional developers and schools. I think Richard DuFour explains it better than anyone, but that's hardly the only work using the "PLC" language, and therefore the definitional confusion ensues. The same is true of words like "rigor" and "relevance," which different people assert (often without much evidence) to mean quite different things.

 What is the best way to use classroom walk-throughs that are not used for evaluating teachers (as per the teachers' contracts) to actually change teaching practices, not simply point out areas for improvement?

 Here are some ideas for maximizing the value of walk-throughs:

First, teachers must feel "set up for success," rather than feeling like they are the victims of an administrator "gotcha!" campaign. This is best accomplished when any observation protocols are public, shared clearly, and practiced by teachers, not just administrators. Some specific focus might be necessary, because most checklists are too exhaustive to be done with care and speed. For example, you might say, "This week, I'm going to focus on two areas—the questioning of students and teacher feedback to students. Examples of particularly good practice in these areas include.... Examples of what is not good professional practice in these areas include...."

Second, if you take notes, do so on *one* piece of paper, and give that paper to the teacher as quickly as possible. Make your purpose clear by saying "this is the only copy of my notes on your walkthrough—it's just coaching, not an official observation or evaluation. I'm not sending it in triplicate to human resources or anywhere else—it's just some ideas to help all of us improve as professionals. Please take a look at my notes. Do they seem to be similar to your own observations?"

Third, be random, fair, and comprehensive. I know one principal who was able to make seven observations of each teacher in the building during the year. Teachers *much* preferred this to the typical single observation of one lesson, which had made the entire year's evaluation based on a single tiny sample of all of the teacher's work.

As a practical matter, principals must do both coaching and evaluation, but done properly, the coaching will help to create better evaluations and fewer problems at the end of the year.

Another idea is to make evaluation a two-way street. When one principal started regular walk-throughs, she also started giving the faculty an opportunity to provide evaluations of her after every faculty meeting and in other electronic and paper feedback mechanisms.

What do you think about the overlap between performance pay systems for teachers and Professional Learning Communities? You said that we must go deeper into the systems we have in place. We are entering our third year of PLCs and our second year using the Alternative Teacher Performance Pay System. As a school leader, what do you think is the best way to approach both systems simultaneously? To me, they seem to have opposite beliefs behind them.

Please see *Hard Facts* by Jeffrey Pfeffer and Robert Sutton. If there is evidence that "performance pay" works, I'll be the first to sign up. But so far, that's not the case. In fact, the opposite is true—paying for high test scores has a counterproductive effect, driving teachers away from high-poverty, high-mobility, and high-challenge schools.

I've attempted to tell this to boards and administrators and have been told, "We don't care—we believe that economic incentives work." I can only suggest that if a person was really motivated by economic incentives, then the choice between investment banking and education would probably not have led in the latter direction.

Q 118 **Where can I find some research about whether good school plans make a real difference? I am a regional director and I feel that I can influence school leaders' work if I can work with them to design good school plans.**

A The Leadership and Learning Center's research on school planning is very extensive, involving more than two thousand schools. I published many of these results in my book *The Learning Leader* (2006). In addition, my colleague Stephen White has a new analysis of the data in his recently published book *Leadership Maps* (2009). Stephen has worked extensively with educational systems to improve their school planning processes.

Our analysis process is called PIM—Planning, Implementation, and Monitoring. We provide a detailed rubric-based review of every school plan in a system, and then provide individualized feedback to each school and to the system-level leadership.

Q 119 **I have heard that you did research that demonstrated an inverse relationship between "pretty" strategic plans and student achievement. Can you provide a citation or reference for this research?**

A My research on "pretty" vs. "ugly" plans is published in my book *The Learning Leader.*

I realize that in public presentations, I'm somewhat tongue-in-cheek about the virtues of "ugly" plans vs. "pretty" plans, but evidence is evidence. The plans that required the greatest conformity to state format requirements (the "pretty" plans) were associated with lower student achievement on twenty-five separate measurements than the plans that had low conformity to format requirements (the "ugly" plans). This is quite similar to the findings of the Prichard Committee for Academic Excellence in Kentucky, which found that while high-performing, high-poverty schools had many qualities in common (similar to my earlier 90/90/90 research), they also were consistent in low compliance with state format requirements for their plans.

The conclusion should not be that planning is a waste of time. Rather, there are very particular qualities of plans that *are* associated with improved achievement—and those qualities are not always what state departments of education require. For example, we found that focus, specificity, and measurability are critical variables of plans that are related to improved student achievement. But states frequently fall prey to what I call the "Prego effect"—whatever buzz words and strategies anyone is looking for, accumulated from decades of initiatives and ideas, they should be in the plan, so that the inspector can exclaim, "It's *in* there!" This leads to long, exhaustive, and unfocused plans. Short, explicit, focused plans are associated with improved achievement. Moreover, we found that frequent monitoring of adult and student actions is essential, as are mid-course corrections (documented in my book *Accountability for Learning*). Mid-course corrections are, of necessity, "ugly" compared to the plans that are embossed and immutable.

I'm concerned about the amount of time school leaders spend on plan format rather than on monitoring, implementation, and appropriate changes to make effective, dynamic plans the living documents that they should be.

I am a school administrator. My superintendent has asked that I concentrate my work at one of our sites in particular that she has concerns about. These concerns are mostly about the capacity of the site administrative team. What has stumped me is that she has asked for me to suggest some quantifiable student outcomes that I can provide her with on a weekly basis to show that my presence at the site is making an impact. My focus on the site began in March. She suggested indictors such as "less referrals being written by the teachers."

I am not sure that is really a student outcome, or that we can expect that number to move much over the time period of a week. Weekly benchmark exams are not in place. There are three district-level benchmark exams but those have already been

given. We have two months left of school. Do you have any suggestions for me?

 How does "administrator presence" relate to "student outcomes" if you don't have clear data from the former that relates to the latter? Perhaps you need to consider some intermediate variables. For example, the administrator (you) influences teacher professional practice (e.g., the quantity of nonfiction writing, the implementation of multiple-method assessment, or the timeliness of feedback). And then those indicators (perhaps on a rubric of 4 to 1) can be related to weekly student results (homework compliance, quiz results, attendance, engagement, etc.).

What specific classroom practices can you influence with just two months left? If I had to select "high-impact" strategies, I'd focus on grading policies and final exam practices. For example, if you just eliminate the zero and the average in grading, you can have a quantitative increase in pass rates this semester. If you move finals up two weeks earlier, and use those results for formative feedback, then let kids re-test using a parallel assessment, you will improve final exam performance.

 At my school, there is only one teacher for each subject at each grade level. I want to know the best way to group my teachers into data teams.

I would propose that we create vertical data teams—for example, science teachers for grades 9–12. The focus could be on universal skills, such as those related to the scientific method.

Can you offer any guidance?

 I like your solution. Here is how I would elaborate on that idea:

To structure your teachers in data teams, you might consider alternating between two types of data teams. The first, as you said, would be same-subject, multi-grade teams—math for grades 9–11; reading for grades 9–12, etc. The issue for these teams is Power Standards—"What do ninth-grade students need to know and be able to do in order to enter tenth grade with confidence and success?" That question is best addressed by an inter-grade dialogue.

The second type of data team would be same-grade, multi-subject groups. These groups could consider, for example, how a nonfiction writing program could be used in math, science, social studies, and literature in the same grade. Here are some questions that a high school science/math/social studies data team might address: "When do science teachers lose instructional time because they are teaching math that students need for proficiency in science? How can math teachers rearrange their curricula to save time for their colleagues? What are relevant problems in history, geography, and economics that lend themselves to math standards (drawing inferences from graphs; creating graphs; recognizing patterns in data) and how could math and social studies have joint assignments that reinforce essential learning?

I am having a problem with a group of teachers in my school who are reluctant to work together as a planning team. This team teaches kindergarten. There are eight teachers. Half of them are bilingual teachers. Six of the teachers are in their first five years of teaching, and the other two teachers are highly experienced, thirty-year teachers who openly say that they cannot learn anything from a planning session with rookie teachers. They say it is a waste of their time, and they want to plan on their own, unless the group is willing to let them lead the planning and to do what they say. They want the meeting to be structured in a way that is a good use of time for all.

My expectation is that all teams meet weekly to discuss learning objectives and lesson plans for the next week, talk about how they will assess student learning, and share ideas and resources. I want teams of teachers discussing curriculum—I feel these discussions help them better understand the objectives and how to assess learning. Currently the group of six less-experienced teachers meets and plans weekly without the two veteran teachers. When the veteran teachers have been "forced" to team plan in the past, they intimidate the others to some extent. The newer teachers are reluctant to voice an opinion, for fear that their ideas will be criticized. Specialists met with the team yesterday to share district feedback from a recent walk-through by the language arts coordinator and the team became defensive and argued with the suggestions, saying "That's not

how it is done in kindergarten." Their data shows that eighty-five percent of their students met the end-of-year reading expectation last year, so I know there is room for improvement.

What do you think our next steps should be? I think we need to focus on data and refine our approach by using protocols, so that all team members contribute (some never utter a word during planning). I spoke to one of the experienced teachers yesterday and he said he is willing to meet with the team "as long as it is a good use of my time." He feels that looking at the week's objectives and assessments is a good conversation that will benefit all teachers.

 The veteran teacher vs. new teacher conflict is quite common. Rather than focusing on the resistance from the veterans, I would encourage you to be incredibly appreciative of the enthusiasm and support of your six newer teachers. Certainly there is some resistance, but it sounds as if the support is far greater than the resistance. That is a credit to you and your leadership team.

In order to encourage persistence in this effort, you should create some short-term wins. Think of ways to use formative assessment, including assessment of students and observations of teachers, to demonstrate with clarity how things are better in December than they were in September. Don't wait until the end of the school year to demonstrate success.

With regard to the kindergarten issue, I'd simply refer to the evidence: The number one predictor of fourth-grade success in literacy and math is kindergarten reading readiness. Therefore, teachers who think that kindergarten is for play and not learning are well-intentioned, but wrong. It is absolutely essential that we focus our kindergarten students on letters, numbers, organization, and a sense of accomplishment. School is not only fun—it's also a place where students experience success. When we "love students to failure," we are not helping them.

This really is an equity issue—wealthy families who send their kids to private kindergartens that cost $25,000 annual tuition expect that their five- and six-year-old kids will read and write. We should expect no less from our poor and minority children. If we fail to have these high expectations, then the gap between rich kids and poor kids will increase. Just this morning I was teaching a group of

English as a Second Language students. I know first-hand how tempting it is to leave them alone, let them be quiet, and not challenge them. But I can't "love them to failure"—I have to challenge them, and I know that my job is not to be popular or nice, but to be effective and help them learn.

This morning, I met with one of our schools' second-grade teams regarding regrouping for English Language Development. I gave a small presentation about the importance of focused, targeted instruction. There are two older, established teachers who do not want to regroup for this vital 45-minute daily block, and two younger teachers who are, therefore, suffering. It is the students who will ultimately pay the price for this nonsense. I am going back next week with the intention of hammering this thing out, so that students are grouped in a manner that will allow focused instruction to take place. This is a power struggle/culture issue. Do you have any suggestions, comments, or nuggets of wisdom for me?

First, consider an action research project—do a "pre-test" and "post-test" that you all agree is fair, and compare the gains of the group that received the extra instruction to the gains of the group that did not. Let the data speak for itself.

Second, if you have a high student turnover rate, or other causes for ambiguous or shifting test results, ask the "What is the risk?" question. In other words, point out "If we give kids extra literacy support and they don't need it, then we risk nothing."

My question concerns communication. It is essential that all players—administrators, teachers, students and parents—are on the same page. Yet this seems to be a major issue in every district I have visited. What have you found to be the most effective way to communicate goals, data, and other information that needs to be disseminated?

There really is not one sure way to communicate with all stakeholders. In fact, the best advice I can offer is that you provide multiple channels of communication, including personal meetings, e-mail, brochures, public meetings, etc. When it comes to parent communication, educational leaders need to do a much better job in many districts of using the parents' home language, not just English, for communications. And I think educators could generally do a better job in *all* communications by reducing the amount of educational jargon involved. I call it the "refrigerator rule"—if your communication isn't clear enough and simple enough to be posted on the door of the refrigerator in the homes of your employees, parents, board members, and other stakeholders, then you probably need to make it more succinct and clear.

I am a principal and a member of the Harvard Principals' Advisory Board. Our school district has identified six extremely high-needs schools that have consistently performed poorly on our state's standards-based assessment. In a dramatic move, the teacher's union and the superintendent came to an agreement to implement drastic changes at these schools. Among these is to remove the principals and bring in new principals that the superintendent has identified as highly effective based upon performance at their schools. I was selected to take on the position of principal at one of these extremely low-performing schools.

I am both honored and a bit nervous about taking on this new challenge. I have read your literature on 90/90/90 schools and on how those administrators and teachers were effective in dramatically increasing student achievement. I have also read your book *The Learning Leader.* I am very excited about your research and your ideas. Nonetheless I go into this challenging venture with a great deal of trepidation. If I fail, it means that the students that I am charged with saving and the teachers and I am charged with developing professionally will be the losers. Failure is just not an option. The students at the school to which I am being reassigned are 98 percent African-American and 96 percent free or reduced lunch. They come from troubled homes in a

troubled community. Their main refuge is the school. Their only hope is the opportunity that can be afforded to them through the public education system. As I move into this school, I feel a profound sense of responsibility. The children, their parents, the teachers, the superintendent, and the school board will all be looking to me to turn things around.

Do you have any words of wisdom or suggestions other that what I've read in your literature? I want to be able to do what is right for these students and help the teachers to know that they and their students need not be considered failures. In short, I want to make a difference, which is the reason I got into this profession more than twenty years ago.

 In highly challenging environments, with disadvantaged children, your relentless enthusiasm, confidence, and optimism will be essential for you and your staff. You will also need to have a laser-like focus on achievement. It's the most important thing in the lives of these kids—literally a lifeline. I think of their literacy as a public health matter that we must take as seriously as we would safety, vaccinations, and medical care. The convenience of adults is a distant second to the needs of these kids, and they need you to be a champion who believes in them. The same will be true of the staff. The core group who will believe in you and give you the benefit of the doubt will need your time and encouragement, and the negative whiners who will engage you in toxic combat will bleed you dry emotionally and physically. So focus your energy on your champions and don't invest a lot of time trying to convert those who won't believe in your children.

I wish you the best of luck on this vital and rewarding journey.

CHAPTER 9

Miscellaneous

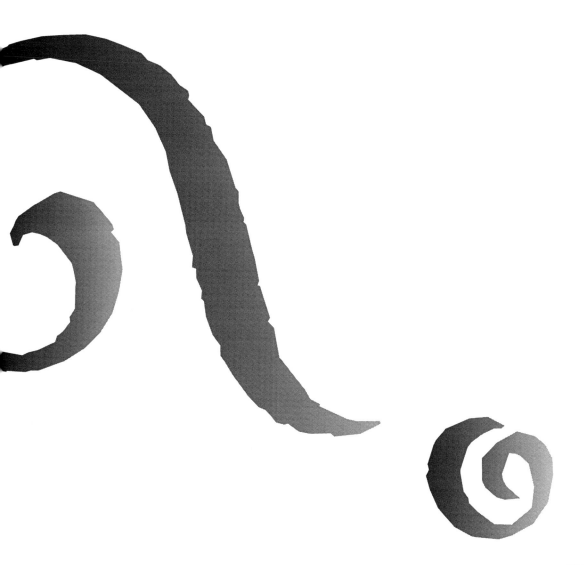

Miscellaneous

I spoke with you briefly about the effectiveness of small schools versus big schools. You said that it is not the size of the school that matters, but whether the teachers make a connection to or develop relationships with their students. In other words, It is whether or not teachers care about their students that matters.

Lately I have been reading some of Deborah Meier's feelings about small schools including *Keeping School : Letters to Families from Principals of Two Small Schools* and Jonathan Kozol's *The Shame of the Nation* about de facto segregated school systems.

I think we become disconnected from the truth by validating schools based upon a single test score or other numerical goals. Don't get me wrong—I know it is important for schools to have good test scores and be considered "passing" schools; to demonstrate adequate yearly progress; to strive to be better than the state and national average. However, we also need schools to teach students to respect, and understand, and tolerate, and debate with dignity, and help, and support, and be a member of a family.

I want to continue to read and learn about what we do wrong, but I also want to grab hold of and write about what we do right, and what we work hard to do. There is a need to change a great deal about education in the United States, and I think those of us in small schools or in financially disadvantaged schools can be on the cutting edge rather than on the butcher's floor.

I, too, greatly respect Kozol and Meier. The question is, "What do we do about it?"

My writing on the subject is clear—do *not* rely on test scores alone, but also consider the actions of school leaders, teachers, parents, and policy makers. My book *The Learning Leader* elaborates on this point.

However feckless policymakers may be, and however disengaged parents and students may be, we can nevertheless make a positive difference for students, including those in poverty, and we *must* do so.

Small schools are fine, but they are no substitute for quality teachers. The size of the school is an insignificant variable compared to the quality of classroom teachers and school leaders.

Could you please direct me to the most convincing and concise data to sway apprehensive staff that your approach is effective?

Consider the following:

1. Teachers *save time* by engaging in collaboration and effective practice. In my studies, the time required for collaborative scoring goes from 45 minutes to 10 minutes when teachers are willing to engage in the challenging and difficult work of collaboration for four consecutive sessions.

2. Teachers *improve discipline* when students are performing at higher levels. Suspensions, disruptions, and academic dishonesty are all lower when you take the steps we recommend to improve student achievement.

3. Teachers have *higher morale* when they can spend more time on thinking, teaching, and meaningful feedback, and less time on discipline, management, and corrective communication.

I've published a good deal of research on these subjects—go to www.LeadandLearn.com for lots of free research downloads. But at the end of the day, ask this question: What would we do if there were no research? What if there were no statistics? What would we do if we only sought to do the right thing?

I would suggest that collaboration, effective feedback and grading, use of standards, and all the things I've suggested in my books and seminars don't need research—they are just moral and ethical things for teachers to do.

Would you ask, "What would I do if my cafeteria managers were apprehensive about new hygiene requirements?" or "What would I do if my crosswalk patrols were apprehensive about new traffic safety requirements?" I don't think you would worry about opposition. You'd say, "We're talking about the safety and health of children! We have to do this—it's a matter of life and death!"

If that's how you would react to apprehension from people in the cafeteria or crosswalk staff, then why wouldn't you take the same view toward literacy, math, science, technology, social studies, and every other subject in school? It's truly a health and safety issue. When kids fail, they have dramatically higher health and safety risks than when they succeed.

I am a third-year Social Studies teacher. I taught at a Title I rural school my first two years, and am now at an urban middle school. This school is not fully Title I, but does qualify for and receive funds for one Title I program for parental involvement activities.

I go back and forth between total frustration and tacit commitment to a seemingly unachievable ideal. I was encouraged by reading your work about the existence of a disadvantaged school that has actually sustained academic excellence over a period of time. I was not surprised, however, that this feat occurred at an elementary school. What about middle schools? This seems to be the "no man's land" of the educational system, especially for low socio-economic schools with diverse populations. It seems to be virtually impossible to get parents to be accountable, to get parents to expect their kids to be accountable, to get students to be accountable, and to get buy-in from teachers, administrators, and parents that it is possible to set high expectations and have students meet them.

Do you know of any middle school that is attempting to implement sustained excellence strategies, and is having any success in their efforts?

I share your frustration with middle schools—it's a great opportunity to make a positive difference for students, yet far too many middle schools have fragmented curricula and, in a vain attempt to "get kids ready for high school," have high demands, high failure rates, and interventions that are inadequate and late.

Fortunately, there are exceptions, and I've documented a number of middle schools that have made exceptional progress in my books *Leading Change in Your Schools, The Learning Leader,* and *Accountability for Learning.* I also include some of them on my DVD series *Data for Learning,* where you can see middle school teachers in high-poverty schools having very productive and professional conversations about how to use formative data to make real-time interventions for kids in need.

None of the solutions are particularly new or surprising—successful middle schools spend more time on reading, assign more nonfiction writing, invoke appropriate consequences for missing work (one of the primary causes of middle school failure) in the form of making students *do the work* rather than giving them zeroes and "F's," and encourage lots and lots of interpersonal relationships with teachers. Most of all, successful middle schools identify kids who are in trouble well before they have accumulated "F's" and multiple course failures, and are 16-year-old eighth-graders.

 I am a principal in a school system that has been using much of your 90/90/90 research in our school improvement plan, and we are really seeing some great progress in our Professional Learning Communities and in our achievement scores. I am also a doctoral candidate, and have been working with some hypotheses that I thought you might be able to help with. I am interested in the long-term outcomes for minority children who *are* successful on standardized tests—in particular, I would like to determine whether or not eliminating the achievement gap will be powerful enough to dismantle, or begin to dismantle, systemic racism in the larger society. Does passing achievement tests correlate with children being empowered to make positive change in their lives and in their communities? Or are we continuing to define success through a dominant culture lens rather than a measure of having the capacity to create a more equitable world?

On a more quantifiable note, has any of your research followed children further into their educational careers and/or lives to determine how things play out for them after they find success at a 90/90/90 school?

 First, on the issue of "dominant culture" tests—I think it is tempting, but dangerous, to join the chorus of criticism here—the Scholastic Aptitude Test (SAT) is biased and racist, and so are tests of all kinds—tests for law school and medical school, the Federal Aviation Administration pilot exam …. But if we stop there, how does that impact the chances of minority kids to be doctors, lawyers, and pilots? Moreover, why doesn't anybody ever say that the tests of baseball, football, and basketball—all Anglo sports until

1945 or so—are barriers to minority students? They can learn complex fifteen-step defensive maneuvers, but they can't learn two-step equations in algebra? They can master a playbook with 200 distinct offences, but can't memorize SAT vocabulary? The real racism isn't in the tests, but in our collective expectations of kids.

Some of the most interesting research on this subject appeared in Richard Sanders' 2004 article "A Systemic Analysis of Affirmative Action in American Law Schools" in *Stanford Law Journal*. It followed students who had been admitted to Ivy league and other top-tier law schools and found, disturbingly, that they had a lower probability of practicing their profession and making partner in a law firm, because of those schools' efforts to avoid "teaching to the test"—in this case, the bar exam. So in an effort to be socially enlightened, these elite law schools managed to put minority students and their families deep into debt, but because they didn't want to buy into the dominant culture of the bar exam, they "helped" these students avoid getting the high-paying jobs that could have created a wealthy class of professionals among previously disenfranchised people.

These findings are as provocative as your question, and I think we need to confront the issues directly. The preponderance of the evidence says that we can and must challenge students, and that they will respond. When we temporize and equivocate, we let them off the hook. What does our educational system, which hesitates to challenge kids in math, science, and English, but willingly challenges them in football, basketball, and baseball, say about our society? Too often, the kids that we hesitate to challenge in math go on to drop out of school and learn to calculate drug deals in grams, ounces, dollars, pesos and euros.

Will we dismantle racism by helping minority students achieve higher test scores? The best hope on this comes from David Perkins, co-director with Howard Gardner of Project Zero at Harvard University from 1972–2000. Perkins (1995) studied how the hated ethnic groups of the day in 1915—Irish and Italians—were found to be inferior races based on their performance on standardized tests. One generation later, in 1937, they scored at the top, and those groups now rule many American cities that, just a century ago, had signs out that said "No dogs or Irish need apply." I am, therefore, incredibly hopeful that some disenfranchised groups will overcome these barriers and become dominant. But that vision will happen only if math and English and science teachers challenge kids and treat them with the same respect that their athletic coaches have already shown for a generation or more, by giving them challenges, accepting no excuses, demanding exceptional effort, and instilling supreme confidence.

For some research on minority students' success after high school, see Vincent Tinto's (1975) work on Latina success in high school, followed by failure in post-secondary education. He has some very provocative findings. We do students (minority female students in particular) no favors by putting them on the honor roll for being quiet, compliant, and nice, and then having them get hammered in college because we failed to give them adequate challenges in high school.

 I read the following excerpt in a newspaper today. I know better than to believe it, but I need some references to give to the reporter who wrote the story. Can you help?

> **"That's critical information, because decades of research shows that socio-demographics have a far bigger impact on test scores than school quality. The so-called achievement gap between white, middle-class students and students who are poor and/or minorities is a national phenomenon that is consistent and substantial."**

 Whoever made the claim that "decades of research" has shown that demographic impact is greater than the impact of school quality must be referring to decades from a few centuries ago, because that subject has been addressed exhaustively in the past thirty years with the following findings:

1. The impact of the classroom teacher on student success accounts for approximately twice the variation in achievement as do the demographic characteristics of the student. Visit www.edTrust.org to read "Good Teaching Matters," by Kati Haycock in *Thinking K–16*. The citations in the article will take you to the original research of Linda Darling-Hammond, among others.

2. Examine the overwhelming power of demographics as a hypothesis to be tested. If it's true, then 100 percent poverty schools can't have high achievement. Of course, research from thirty years ago by Ronald Edmonds at Michigan State University, (1979) and all of my more recent research on 90/90/90 schools, published in *Accountability in Action, Accountability for Learning,* and many articles in *Educational Leadership,* prove that the above hypothesis is false.

3. The retort to the above evidence is that "those are just isolated examples." Putting aside for a moment the fact that logically it requires only *one* case to disprove a hypothesis, there are *many* examples, and they are growing in number. See the "Dispelling the Myth" section at www.edTrust.org to see multiple examples. See Karin Chenoweth's *It's Being Done* (2007) for more of the same. See www.springboardschools.org for more high-poverty, high-performing schools.

This is not about "dueling experts" but about the truth—you have the facts on your side.

I am the math coach at a Title I school. I have been able to share your research with our school staff. We are all working hard to acquire 90/90/90 status by helping our students reach proficient levels.

I am also a doctoral student. I would really like to do more research on using effective data analysis to close the achievement gap at high poverty schools. Your work is very inspirational to me. Do you have any research suggestions?

My primary advice to any doctoral student is to *narrow the focus.* You can write fifty books on high poverty schools. Only one of those books needs to be your dissertation, and the sooner you finish that, the sooner you can begin work on the other forty-nine books.

Therefore, I recommend that you select a *very* specific topic— such as fourth grade English as a Second Language students who are having difficulty with math problem solving—and then work *in depth* on that topic.

My other recommendation is that you find a support group of

other doctoral students who will agree to "walk" together to receive your degrees. Before the final "walk," you agree to a weekly "walk"— a meeting at your homes, a bookstore, or a coffee shop. *Every* week for a year, you all agree to bring one article summary to the meeting, with a complete citation and *exact* quotations. If five people do this for fifty weeks, you will have 250 references, all focused on the same areas of interest. The difference between the large number of people who don't finish their dissertations and the small number who do is not intelligence or ability—it is organization and structure and social support systems.

Q 132

I am planning to write my dissertation on high poverty/high performing schools. Can you recommend books and articles that could guide me? I am really hoping to make an impact with this work.

A

From my work, I would suggest the books *Accountability in Action* (2004, 2nd ed.), *Accountability for Learning* (2004), *The Learning Leader* (2006), and *Leading Change in Your School* (2009).

I also recommend John Hattie's *Visible Learning* (2009) and Karin Chenoweth's *It's Being Done* (2007). See also Chenoweth's excellent article in *Kappan* (2009).

Hattie's book is particularly good, as it allows you to evaluate the relative impact of demographic characteristics and teaching interventions.

Q 133

I am presently working on my doctorate, and I need help finding a topic for my dissertation research. I love your work with assessment and leadership, and I am especially interested in assessment, staff development, and student leadership, and in Stephen Covey's *Seven Habits of Highly Effective People*.

A

Here is the best advice you will receive about your dissertation: It is your *next* piece of research, not your *last* piece of research.

The fields you have described are vast, and you could—and probably should—write many books about those areas in your lifetime. In fact, I encourage people pursuing a doctorate to make a list of the fifty books they would like to write, ending with *Advice to My Great-Great-Grandchildren.*

The first book on that list is your dissertation. It is imperative that you narrow the focus of your work. Rather than "assessment" for example, you might want to write about "the impact of formative assessment on problem-solving skills among high-poverty fifth graders."

Narrow the focus, finish the dissertation, then do what Covey did and write a bunch of other books.

I am a high school principal. I have read your books, and attended some of your presentations and seminars. We have taken your advice and have made great strides.

After reviewing our data from the past school year, it appears our greatest challenge is graduation rate. In our school, approximately forty percent of the students are below the poverty index. The drop-outs for the past three years appear to be primarily among students who were older than usual in ninth grade. We have thirty-nine students in the ninth grade who are at least six months older than their classmates. These thirty-nine students are at risk of not advancing, so we have implemented a curriculum that accelerates their learning and provides them with an opportunity to graduate on time.

We are having a debate concerning the impact of students coming to high school at the appropriate age, versus not coming until their learning is "at grade level." In your opinion, what should the determining factor be for making this decision in elementary and middle school? I have learned that graduation rate is a K–12 problem that must be discussed at all grade levels.

I think you have already answered your own question. If a disproportionate number of drop-outs are older than their classmates, then you have evidence that making students repeat grades is not working. I'm willing to endorse just about any strategy to motivate under-performing students short of water-boarding, but I do insist that the strategy be supported by evidence. When teachers say, "We need to punish them, flunk them, retain them, and hurt them, because that's the only way that they will learn personal responsibility," and then the students who are subjected to this thoughtful educational approach drop out of school and go directly to jail, the evidence does not support that strategy. Of course, social promotion is also not a good solution. Bleeding-heart educators that tell kids that they are OK when, in fact, they can't read, don't solve the problem, either. So what's the solution? Here the evidence is clear—intensive intervention. See my article "Teachers Step Up" in the September 2007 issue of *Educational Leadership* for the tip of the iceberg of evidence on this point. Teachers should *demand* more work, more time, and more success. It's not popular, but it works. Social promotion and retention do not work.

I recently attended a conference at which you mentioned that you think the use of Wikipedia and Google is making us (and our students) stupid.

I disagree. I think that this idea stems from confusion about the difference between the concepts of "tool" and "skill." The nature of the issue is completely different if we want to discuss the reliability of Wikipedia, i.e. Wikipedia as a tool, than if we want to discuss the kind of use that students in general make of resources like Wikipedia in their learning.

In many cases, students' use of Wikipedia is excellent. Students use it as what it is, a tertiary source that can provide a possible point of entrance to a topic—from Wikipedia, students follow the suggested links to get to some real evidence from an original source. I have also seen terrible uses of Wikipedia (such as using it as the source for Newton's second law, as if Wikipedia was the place where Newton wrote his *Philosophiae Naturalis Principia Mathematica*). However, when you read such essays, it is also very likely that the student will have cited only one book as a source, most of the time the text book used in class.

This brings me to my second point: The use of *all* types of resources for research is a skill to be taught, developed, and practiced in the classroom, and what could be better than discussing with students what kind of sources are suitable and why, including *any* encyclopedias and *any* wikis? After your conference, I discussed this issue with several teachers, and at least two of them told me they just tell their students not to use Wikipedia. This does not seem to be a good way to exercise and develop students' critical thinking skills.

Regarding the use of Wikipedia as a source, Wikipedia itself offers links to several investigations done on its reliability, some very positive and some plainly negative. One of the studies about Wikipedia, conducted by *Nature* magazine, reached the conclusion that the number of mistakes on Wikipedia are of the same order as those in Encyclopedia Britannica. And it is not without reason that Encarta closed down.

And then there are the advantages of Wikipedia—it is readily accessible at any time, in many languages, and has information about almost every conceivable topic, for free.

Despite the usual comments coming from the area of humanities about the unreliability of Wikipedia articles, in the fields of science and mathematics, there is almost no opposition to its reliability. I think that this disparity is intrinsically connected with the nature of the knowledge in those different fields. People from around the world cannot come to agreement on highly sensitive and subjective topics like the concepts and definitions of democracy, religion, and ethics, etc.

Wikipedia, as a product of our culture, developed by people all over the world, will, and actually *must* reflect not only the knowledge that we have accumulated, but also the pending debates that are part of our world. What could be better than to prepare our students to take part in those debates? That would require us, as teachers, to help students develop their critical thinking skills, which clearly includes helping them understand that *any* source—book, encyclopedia, or newspaper—should always be read with a sort of skepticism. Science text books are full of mistakes, and students have been using them for ages.

I also object to your comment about Google making us stupid. I think it can be used wisely, and therefore I think the skills necessary to use it wisely can and must be taught. Any search engine can be used to find a needle in a haystack, or to be passively guided about what to read. Search engines are not to be blamed if a student uses them by typing in a concept and then following the first three links provided. That is not Google's fault; it is actually *our* fault as teachers.

Your criticisms of Encyclopedia Britannica and other sources are quite true. All of them—wikis and the references that they seek to emulate—offer just hypotheses, not facts. I require my students to go to original sources—to test the hypothesis forwarded by Wikipedia or Encyclopedia Britannica or any other source. What I cannot tolerate is the "cutting and pasting" masquerading as "research"—it's just lazy.

I think that your inference about how teachers in sciences and humanities view Wikipedia is interesting. You contend that science teachers like Wikipedia and humanities teachers do not. My observation would be quite the opposite—Wikipedia gives a forum to anti-science zealots who have a political or religious agenda, allowing them to masquerade that agenda as fact. There are documented cases of people claiming to be "professors" and "researchers" who are simply hacks promoting a political or religious viewpoint. Think of Peter Steiner's 1993 cartoon in *The New Yorker*, in which a canine is typing on a computer and saying, "On the Internet, nobody knows you're a dog." It's the same on Wikipedia—there is not a distinction between allegations and evidence. I already know the response: "We have volunteer editors and they will fix mistakes." The problem is that once something is published, it is cut and pasted everywhere. Wikipedia's corrections and edits only happen in their environment—they do not fix the errors that have been cut and pasted elsewhere.

With regard to Google, you are quite right—it is not the fault of Google that the people conducting searches are not very careful. What I had attempted to suggest was that searchers must be more precise—getting two million hits is not a sign of an abundance of information, but a sign of a poorly constructed search. As I attempted to say, "A little more Socrates" would help most students conduct better searches.

We both have the same objective—students who think and express their ideas with critical reasoning. I simply want my students to be as critical of Google and Wikipedia as they are of me.

Why do most world-class athletes have birthdays in January, February, or March?

This observation was made by Steven Levitt and Stephen Dubner, authors of *Freakonomics*. What could possibly account for the disproportionate number of elite athletes in Europe who are in the most elite leagues whose birthdays are early in the year? Could it be that astrology is true, conferring on the winter sun signs special prowess? There is a more mundane explanation, and it starts very early in life. At so-called "talent development" camps, limited numbers of very young players are recruited to receive top coaching and training. The coach has a limited number of spaces to allocate to these potential superstars of tomorrow. Who will get the nod? The cut-off for age-range eligibility is December 31. The coach can choose anyone from the age bracket, but those born in January and February are ten to eleven months older, more experienced, stronger, more coordinated, more socially adept at dealing with other players, and more knowledgeable of the rules. Does this make the Aquarians more talented than the Scorpios? Believers in astrology make this inference, but a more logical conclusion is that we have a self-fulfilling prophecy at work. Kids who have a slight advantage conferred by age and experience will, as a result, be selected for talent development, and therefore they will receive the very best in training and support, and will become elite athletes. But it was the accident of birth date, not astrology or innate talent alone, that played a role in their success.

The relationship of this phenomenon to education is quite meaningful, I think, because many teachers regard their primary job as confirming the presumptions of parents and noticing the skills and experiences that students already have. What do teachers do when they think that they have "talent development" students in reading, math, and science? The 1960s Pygmalion Effect research done by Robert Rosenthal and Lenore Jacobson, and the more recent observations in *Freakonomics*, suggest that these selections lead coaches and teachers to reinforce assumptions of success.

See also Carol Dweck's work at Stanford, reflected in her book *Mindset: The New Psychology of Success*—she found that students who believe that their intellect can be improved do better, again supporting the self-fulfilling prophecy idea.

I have read your statements about how boys and video games seem to click. What's your suggestion on how to get girls to create and play electronic games? There is a large gender gap in this area.

 Although boys do play video games a great deal, there are qualities of those games that are not gender-specific and that I think can be used to engage girls as well. For example, I remember a school in which the students were using Flash 8 to create their own video games, and that creative process is as inviting to girls as it is to boys. Moreover, the instant feedback feature of video games is also appealing to girls—in fact, girls' appreciation of praise and reinforcement is as strong as, or stronger than, that of boys. Finally, a big part of engagement is not so much the technical sophistication, but the element of choice. Boys and girls both appreciate the freedom to make choices and the opportunity for variety, sometimes with a complex combination of individuality and imitation.

My own experience and a good deal of education literature suggest that we can learn a great deal by experimentation and by asking students themselves what would interest them. There have been projects that I thought were pretty pedestrian that engaged my students, and there have been projects that I would have bet the farm were exciting and engaging that my students found dull. Teaching is a constant challenge requiring experimentation and professional reflection.

 I have a question about sub-grouping. Why is it important to distinguish students who are above/on/below grade level by race? If I have two students who have trouble with comprehension, why is it important whether they are African-American or Caucasian? Truthfully, no two kids are alike. None of my students have the exact same family life or the exact same heritage. I find it offensive that I am forced to look at my students in this way. Their similarities in the classroom appear when the children have difficulty with a particular skill. I know from my data that I have four students who have trouble with sequencing events in a story, and their race doesn't drive my

instruction. The only sub-group that interests me is English Language Learner. Knowing that English isn't spoken at home is useful to guide instruction. Can you help me to understand the benefit of sub-grouping my data?

A There are two issues here. First is the one you raise—if a student needs help in math or reading, what difference does it make what his or her race is? There is not "African-American algebra" or "Hispanic geometry" instruction—let's just give all students *good* algebra and *good* geometry instruction. Therefore, when the issue is planning curriculum, assessment, and effective teaching strategies, you are absolutely correct—the only "subgroups" that matters are "those who have met the standard" and "those who need additional help."

The second issue, however, is at the heart of equity. If we do not acknowledge that there are differences based on gender, race, economic status, and language, then we will never admit that there is a problem. Call it "Educational 12-step"—the first step is saying, "Hi, I'm Doug, and even though I'm not a bigot, I've got to admit that poor and minority kids in my classroom are performing at a level well below their white and economically advantaged counterparts. I'm not saying that this is my fault, but I *am* admitting that it's a problem, and that I've got to be part of the solution."

The result of this two-level conversation will not, I hope, be to create separate math programs for minority kids. Rather, you should create specific interventions for *any* student who needs help. And conducting the gender, economic, and ethnic analysis should make you realize that if you fail to intervene, your failures disproportionately hurt poor and minority students.

Q 139

Can you please explain the consequences and harmful effects of unequal financing of public education? What types of statistics and facts are available to make this point? Why is it better to have a well-educated public? How does this benefit society as a whole? And what are the potential economic ramifications?

A The consequences are devastating. Here are the facts:

Despite many, many lawsuits about equal financing for education, evidence from Allan Odden and colleagues at the

University of Wisconsin (2009) documents widespread financial disparities among school systems. And that's only what is publicly disclosed. There is a great deal of "off-the-books" funding. Wealthy suburban schools can say, "Need an art teacher? No problem—let's have a society gala, raise $100,000, and hire an art teacher." Poor schools can't get money for hamburgers for the Parent Teachers Association lunch.

But it's much more than financing. Even if the financing were equalized, the distribution of other assets, such as teacher quality, curriculum, assessment, and leadership, are vastly unequal. A study by Yuan and Moreno published in *Educational Researcher* revealed that schools with concentrations of poor Anglo, African-American, and Latino/Hispanic kids are half as likely to have subject-matter certified teachers as are schools with concentrations of middle class Anglo kids, and one-third as likely to have Advanced Placement opportunities. The same is true with leadership—the poorest schools get the newest and least experienced leaders. Wealthy schools get leaders with decades of experience and exceptional quality.

So, money is important, but not sufficient. Even if you triple per-pupil funding in poor schools, if kids there get new and inexperienced teachers, and kids in another, more desirable area get experienced and qualified teachers, you won't have solved the problem.

As for society ramifications, check out www.edTrust.org. Each kid who drops out of school has a $2 million lifetime loss in earnings. We've tripled spending on prisons in the past 15 years—something we always manage to find money for—yet the predictors of the prison population are found in kids that we under-serve in school in poor urban areas.

Frankly, we need to address this as a public health issue. There was a time, fifty years ago, when the nation committed itself to eradicating polio. We didn't just do vaccinations in white suburbs, but vaccinated *every* kid, rich and poor, black, white, and brown. And we succeeded. Kids with iron lungs or leg braces are much less common today. Why can't we have a similar universal commitment to literacy and school success?

Equalization of school finding is necessary, but not sufficient. We must equalize access to *all* the assets that make for great education, including teaching, leadership, curriculum, assessment, and environment.

I teach in a Ph.D. program in Educational Technology. As part of the doctoral requirements, learners conduct independent studies on social change, human development, and systems change. They write knowledge acquisition modules including theory, current research in educational technology, and application of both to a project they identify.

I think your 2009 book *Leading Change in Your School* might be a good addition to readings on theory for either social change, systems change, or both. I know I can recommend your book for the application section of these knowledge acquisition modules. However, in order to use your book for a theoretical investigation in what we call the "breadth" section of these knowledge acquisition modules, I would like to know your perspective as to whether or not you consider yourself to be a theorist, and if you would categorize your book as theory.

I am certainly not qualified as a theorist—there are only a few of those in any century, and I know I am not among them. I am a teacher, a practitioner, and a researcher. I also attempt to be an interpreter of research, in order to make it accessible to others. I fear that much of theory and research has been reduced to prose that is deliberately impenetrable so that only academics, and not practitioners, can read it. Certainly my work is no more than a pebble on the mountain of research in my field.

If my work has value, it is always in the context of others, not alone. Consider different perspectives and methodologies. I'm a quantitative researcher, but readers have much to gain from considering the perspective of case studies (John Goodlad), meta-analysis (Robert Marzano), and meta-meta-analysis (John Hattie). When different researchers of different generations and different methodologies agree, then there is perhaps something there worthy of consideration.

Probably the most valuable section of each of my books is the reference list that offers acknowledgment to other authors.

Bibliography

Ainsworth, L. & Viegut, D. (2006). *Common formative assessments: How to connect standards-based instruction and assessment.* Thousand Oaks, CA: Corwin Press.

Ainsworth, L. (2003a). *Power standards: Identifying the standards that matter the most.* Englewood, CO: Advanced Learning Press.

Ainsworth, L. (2003b). *"Unwrapping" the standards: A simple process to make standards manageable.* Englewood, CO: Advanced Learning Press.

Black, S. (2002). The well-rounded student: Extracurricular activities and academic performance go hand in hand. *American School Board Journal, 189*(6), 33–35.

Calkins, L. M. (1994). *The art of teaching writing* (2nd ed.). Portsmouth, NH: Heinemann.

Capella, E., & Weinstein, R. S. (2001, December). Turning around reading achievement: Predictors of high school students' academic resilience. *Journal of Educational Psychology, 93*(4), 758–771.

Chenoweth, K. (2009, September). It can be done, it's being done, and here's how, *Phi Delta Kappan, 91*(01), pp. 38–43.

Chenoweth, K. (2007). *It's being done: Academic success in unexpected schools.* Cambridge, MA: Harvard Education Press.

Coles, G. (2003). *Reading the naked truth: literacy, legislation, and lies.* Portsmouth, NH: Heinemann.

Covey, S. R. (2004). *The 8th habit: From effectiveness to greatness.* New York: Free Press.

Danielson, C. (2006). *Teacher Leadership That Strengthens Professional Practice.* Alexandria, VA: Association for Supervision and Curriculum Development.

Darling-Hammond, L. (2007, August/September). The Flat Earth and Education: How America's Commitment to Equity Will Determine Our Future, *Educational Researcher, 36*(6), 318–334.

Darling-Hammond, L. (1997). *The right to learn: A blueprint for creating schools that work.* San Francisco: Jossey-Bass.

DuFour, R. (2002). The learning-centered principal. *Educational Leadership, 59*(8), 12–15.

DuFour, R., DuFour, R., & Eaker, R. (2008). *Revisiting professional learning communities at work: New insights for improving schools.* Bloomington, IN: Solution Tree.

Dufour, R., DuFour, R., Eaker, R., & Karhanek, G. (2004). *Whatever it takes: How professional learning communities respond when kids don't learn.* Bloomington, IN: National Educational Service.

DuFour, R., Eaker, R., & DuFour R. (2005). *On common ground: The power of professional learning communities.* Bloomington, IN: National Educational Service.

DuFour, R., Eaker, R., & Many, T. (2006). *Learning by doing: A handbook for professional learning communities at work.* Bloomington, IN: Solution Tree.

Dweck, C. S. (2006). *Mindset: The new psychology of success.* New York: The Random House Publishing Group.

Edmonds, R. (1979, September). Effective Schools for the Urban Poor. *Educational Leadership 37*(1), 15–24.

Fredricks, J. A., & Eccles, J. S. (2006). Is extracurricular participation associated with beneficial outcomes? Concurrent and longitudinal relations. *Developmental Psychology, 42*(4), 698–713.

Fujita, K. (2006). The effects of extracurricular activities on the academic performance of junior high students. *Undergraduate Research Journal for the Human Sciences, 5.* Available: www.kon.org/urc/v5/fujita.html.

Garan, E. (2002). *Resisting reading mandates: How to triumph with the truth.* Portsmouth, NH: Heinemann.

Goodlad, J. I. (1984). *A place called school.* New York: McGraw-Hill Book Co.

Graham, S., & Perin, D. (2007, August.) A meta-analysis of writing instruction for adolescent students." *Journal of Educational Psychology, 99*(3), pp. 445–446.

Guskey, T. R. (2005). Five key concepts kick off the process. *Journal of Staff Development, 26*(1), 36–40.

Guskey, T. R. (2005). *Benjamin S. Bloom: Portraits of an educator.* Lanham, Maryland: Rowman & Littlefield.

Guskey, T. R. (2002). *How's My Kid Doing? A Parents' Guide to Grades, Marks, and Report Cards.* San Francisco: Jossey Bass

Guskey, T. R. (2000). *Evaluating professional development.* Thousand Oaks, Calif.: Corwin Press, Inc.

Guskey, T. R. (2000, December). Grading policies that work against standards ... and how to fix them. *NASSP Bulletin, 84*(620), 20–29.

Guskey, T. R., & Bailey, J. M. (2001). *Developing Grading and Reporting Systems for Student Learning.* Thousand Oaks, CA: Corwin Press.

Guskey, T. R., & Erkens, C. (2009) *The teacher as assessment leader.* Bloomington, IN: Solution Tree.

Hargreaves, A., & Fink, D. (2006). *Sustainable leadership.* San Francisco: Jossey-Bass.

Hattie, J. (2009). *Visible learning: A synthesis of over 800 meta-analyses relating to achievement.* New York: Routledge

Haycock, K. (1998, Summer). Good teaching matters: How well-qualified teachers can close the gap. Thinking K-16, A Publication of *The Education Trust. 3*(2), 1–16.

Haycock, K. (1999). *Dispelling the myth: High-poverty schools exceeding expectations.* Washington, DC: The Education Trust.

Holloway, J. H. (2002). Extracurricular activities and student motivation. *Educational Leadership, 60*(1), 80–81.

Kiuhara, S. A., Graham, S., & Hawken, L. S. (2009, February). Teaching writing to high school students: A national survey. *Journal of educational psychology, 101*(1),136-160.

King, S. (2002). *On writing: A memoir of the craft.* New York: Pocket Books.

Klentschy, M., Garrison, L., & Amaral, O. M. (2000). Valle Imperale Project in Science (VIPS), Four-year comparison of student achievement data 1995–1999. National Science Foundation Grant #ESI-9731274.

Kozol, J. (2005). *The shame of the nation: The restoration of apartheid schooling in America.* New York: Crown Publishers.

Levine, M. (2003). *The myth of laziness.* New York: Simon and Schuster.

Levine, M. (2002). *A mind at a time.* New York: Simon and Schuster.

Levitt, S. D., & Dubner, S. J. (2006). *Freakonomics: A rogue economist explores the hidden side of everything.* New York: HarperCollins Publishers.

Marshall, K. (2005, June). It's time to rethink teacher supervision and evaluation. *Phi Delta Kappan. 86*(10), 727–735.

Marzano, R. J. (Ed.). (2010). *On excellence in teaching.* Bloomington, IN: Solution Tree Press.

Marzano, R. J. (2009, September). Setting the record straight on high-yield strategies. *Phi Delta Kappan, 91*(6), 30–37.

Marzano, R. J. (2009a). *Designing & teaching learning goals & objectives.* Bloomington, IN: Marzano Research Laboratory.

Marzano, R. J. (2009b). *Formative assessment and standards-based grading: Classroom strategies that work.* Bloomington, IN: Solution Tree.

Marzano, R. J. (2007). *The art and science of teaching: A comprehensive framework for effective instruction.* Alexandria, VA: ASCD.

Marzano, R. J. (2006). *Classroom assessment and grading that work.* Alexandria, VA: Association for Supervision and Curriculum Development.

Marzano, R. J. (2003). *What works in schools: Translating research into action.* Alexandria, VA: Association for Supervision and Curriculum Development.

Marzano, R. J. (2001a). *Designing a new taxonomy of educational objectives.* Thousand Oaks, CA: Corwin Press.

Marzano, R. J. (2001b). *A handbook for classroom instruction that works.* Alexandria, VA: Association for Supervision and Curriculum Development.

Marzano, R. J. (2000). *Transforming classroom grading.* Alexandria, VA: Association for Supervision and Curriculum Development.

Marzano, R. J., & Haystead, M. W. (2008). *Making standards useful in the classroom.* Alexandria, VA: Association for Supervision and Curriculum Development.

Marzano, R. J., & Kendall, J. S. (2008). *Designing and assessing educational objectives: Applying the new taxonomy.* Thousand Oaks, CA: Corwin Press.

Marzano, R. J., & Kendall, J. S. (2006). *The new taxonomy of educational objectives,* (2nd ed.) Thousand Oaks, CA: Corwin Press.

Marzano, R. J., & Kendall, J. S. (1998). *Implementing standards-based education (student assessment series).* Washington, DC: National Educational Association.

Marzano, R. J., & Kendall, J. S. (1996). *A comprehensive guide to designing standards-based districts, schools, and classrooms.* Alexandria, VA: Association for Supervision and Curriculum Development.

Marzano, R. J., & Pickering, D. (2007). The case for and against homework. *Educational Leadership, 64*(6), 74–79.

Marzano, R. J., Pickering, D., & Pollock, J. E. (2001). *Classroom instruction that works: Research-based strategies for increasing student achievement.* Alexandria, VA: Association for Supervision and Curriculum Development.

Marzano, R. J., & Waters, T. W. (2009). *District leadership that works: Striking the right balance.* Bloomington, IN: Solution Tree.

Marzano, R. J., Waters, T. W., & McNulty, B. A. (2005). *School leadership that works: From research to results.* Alexandria, VA: Association for Supervision and Curriculum Development.

Meier, D., Sizer, P., & Sizer, N. F. (2004). *Keeping school: Letters to families from principals of two small schools.* Boston: Beacon Press.

Morgan, G. A., Griego, O. V., & Gloeckner, G. (2001). *Introduction to SPSS: An introduction to use and interpretation in research.* Mahwah, New Jersey: Lawrence Erlbaum.

O'Connor, K. (2009). *How to grade for learning K–12* (3rd ed.). Thousand Oaks, CA: Corwin Press.

O'Connor, K. (2007). *A repair kit for grading: 15 fixes for broken grades.* Portland, OR: Educational Testing Service.

O'Connor, K. (2007). The last frontier: Tackling the grading dilemma, In Reeves, D. (Ed.), *Ahead of the Curve: The Power of Assessment to Transform Teaching and Learning,* Bloomington, IN: Solution Tree.

O'Connor, K. (2002). How to grade for learning: Linking grades to standards (2nd ed.). Glenview, IL: Pearson Education.

Odden, A. R. & Archibald, S. (2009). *Doubling student performance … and finding the resources to do it.* Thousand Oaks, CA: Corwin Press.

Patterson, K., Grenny, J., Maxfield, D., McMillan, R., & Switzler, A. (2008). *Influencer: The power to change anything.* New York: McGraw-Hill.

Patterson, M. (2005, May). Hazed! *Educational Leadership, 62*(8), 20-23.

Perkins, D. N. (1995). *Outsmarting IQ: the emerging science of learnable intelligence.* New York: Free Press.

Pfeffer, J. & Sutton, R. I. (2006). *Hard facts, dangerous half-truths and total nonsense: Profiting from evidence-based management.* Boston: Harvard Business School Publishing.

Pink, D. H. (2009). *Drive: The surprising truth about what motivates us.* New York: Riverhead Books.

Reeves, D. B. (2009). *Leading change in your school: How to conquer myths, build commitment, and get results.* Alexandria, VA: Association for Supervision and Curriculum Development.

Reeves, D. B. (2008). *Assessing educational leaders: Evaluating performance for improved individual and organizational results* (2nd ed.). Thousand Oaks, CA: Corwin Press.

Reeves, D. B. (2008, February). Effective grading practices. *Educational Leadership, 65*(5), 85–87.

Reeves, D. B. (2008). *Reframing teacher leadership to improve your school.* Alexandria, VA: Association for Supervision and Curriculum Development.

Reeves, D. B. (Ed.). (2007). *Ahead of the curve: The power of assessment to transform teaching and learning.* Bloomington, IN: Solution Tree.

Reeves, D. B. (2007, November). How do you sustain excellence? *Educational Leadership, 65*(3), 86–87.

Reeves, D. B. (2007, September). Teachers step up. *Educational Leadership, 65*(1), 87–88.

Reeves, D. B. (2006, November). Preventing 1,000 Failures. *Educational Leadership, 64*(3), 88–89.

Reeves, D. B. (2006). *The learning leader: How to focus school improvement for better results.* Alexandria, VA: Association for Supervision and Curriculum Development.

Reeves, D. B. (2006, February). The mad, mad world of education research. *The Education Gadfly, 6*(6). Retrieved March 30, 2010 from www.edexcellence.net/gadfly/index.cfm?issue=228#a2673.

Reeves, D. B. (2006). DVD. Data for learning: A blueprint for improving student achievement using data teams. Englewood, CO: Advanced Learning Press.

Reeves, D. B. (2005). *Accountability in action: A blueprint for learning organizations* (2nd ed.). Englewood, CO: Advanced Learning Press.

Reeves, D. B. (2004). *Accountability for learning: How teachers and school leaders can take charge.* Alexandria, VA: Association for Supervision and Curriculum Development.

Reeves, D. B. (2004). The case against the zero. *Phi Delta Kappan, 86*(4), 324–325.

Reeves, D. B. (2003). High Performance in High Poverty Schools: 90/90/90 and Beyond. Denver, CO: Center for Performance Assessment.

Reeves, D. B. (2002). *101 Questions and answers about standards, assessment, and accountability.* Englewood, CO: Advanced Learning Press.

Reeves, D. B. (2002). *The daily disciplines of leadership: How to improve student achievement, staff motivation, and personal organization.* San Francisco: Jossey-Bass.

Reeves, D. B. (2002). *The leader's guide to standards: A blueprint for educational equity and excellence.* San Francisco: Jossey-Bass.

Reeves, D. B. (2002). *Reason to write: Help your child succeed in school and in life through better reasoning and clear communication.* New York: Simon & Schuster.

Reeves, D. B. (2002). *Reason to write: Student handbook.* New York: Simon & Schuster.

Reeves, D. B. (2002). *Making standards work: How to implement standards-based assessments in the classroom, school, and district* (3rd ed.). Denver, CO: Advanced Learning Press.

Reeves, D. B. (2001). *101 questions & answers about standards, assessment, and accountability.* Denver, CO: Advanced Learning Press.

Reeves, D. B. (2001, June 6). If you hate standards, learn to love the bell curve. *Education Week, 20*(39), 38–39, 52.

Reeves, D. B. (2001). *Crusade in the classroom: How George W. Bush's education reforms will affect your children, our schools.* New York: Simon & Schuster.

Rosenthal, R., & Jacobson, L. (1968). *Pygmalion in the classroom: teacher expectation and pupil's intellectual development.* New York: Holt, Rinehart & Winston.

Sander, R. (2004). A systemic analysis of affirmative action in American law schools. 57 *Stanford Law Review* 367.

Schlechty , P. C. (2009). *Leading for learning: How to transform schools into learning organizations.* San Francisco: Jossey-Bass.

Schmoker, M. (2006). *Results now: How we can achieve unprecedented improvements in teaching and learning.* Alexandria, VA: Association for Supervision and Curriculum Development.

Schmoker, M. (2005). No turning back: The ironclad case for professional learning communities. In R. Dufour, R. Eaker, & R. DuFour (Eds.), *On Common Ground: The Power of Professional Learning Communities.* Bloomington, IN: Solution Tree.

Schmoker, M. J. (2004). Tipping point: From feckless reform to substantive instructional improvement. *Phi Delta Kappan, 85*(6), 424–432.

Schmoker, M. J. (2001). *The results fieldbook: Practical strategies from dramatically improved schools.* Alexandria, VA: Association for Supervision and Curriculum Development.

Schmoker, M. (2001, October 24). The Crayola curriculum. *Education Week, 21*(8), 42–44.

Schmoker, M. J. (1999). *Results: The key to continuous school improvement* (2nd ed.). Alexandria, VA: Association for Supervision and Curriculum Development.

Slavin, R. E., & Fashola, O. (1998). *Show me the evidence! Proven and promising programs for America's schools.* Thousand Oaks, CA: Corwin Press.

Stiggins, R. J. (2007). *Introduction to student-involved assessment for learning* (5th ed.). Upper Saddle River, NJ: Prentice Hall.

Stiggins, R. J. (2000). *Student-involved classroom assessment* (3rd ed.). Upper Saddle River, NJ: Prentice Hall.

Stiggins, R. J., Arter. J., Chappuis J., & Chappuis, S. (2004). *Classroom assessment for student learning: Doing it right, using it well.* Portland, OR: Assessment Training Institute.

Taberski, S., & Harwayne, S. (2000). *On solid ground: Strategies for teaching reading K–3.* Portsmouth, NH: Heinemann.

Tinto, V. (1975). Dropout from higher education: A theoretical synthesis of recent research. *Review of Educational Research, 45*(1), 89–125.

Tucker, M. S., & Codding, J. B. (1998). *Standards for our schools: how to set them, measure them, and reach them.* San Francisco: Jossey-Bass Publishers.

White, S. (2009). *Leadership maps.* Englewood, CO: Lead + Learn Press.

Wiggins, G. (1998). *Educative assessment: Designing assessments to inform and improve student performance.* San Francisco: Jossey-Bass.

Wiggins, G. (1991, February). Standards, Not Standardization. *Educational Leadership, 48*(5), 18–25.

Wiggins, G. & McTighe, J. (2005). *Understanding by design.* Alexandria, VA: Association for Supervision and Curriculum.

Yun, J. T., & Moreno, J. F. (2006, January-February).College access, K–12 concentrated disadvantage, and the next 25 years of education research. *Educational Researcher, 35*(1), 12–19.

Webography

ASCD (formerly the Association for Supervision and Curriculum Development): www.ascd.org

American Association of School Administrators: www.aasa.org

Education Trust: www.edTrust.org

Education Week: www.edweek.org

Inform.com article on single-gender classrooms: inform.com/special-interests/singlesex-classes-praised-levels-602197a

National Association of Secondary School Principals: www.principals.org

Springboard Schools article: *Balancing Act: Best Practices in the Middle Grades* (PDF; Outside Source), (Executive Summary). San Francisco: Springboard Schools, Spring 2007, p. 3.
Available: www.springboardschools.org/research/studies/MSBP-ES.pdf

The Leadership and Learning Center: www.LeadandLearn.com

Index